1000 JAPANESE ONOMATOPOEIA

William de Lange

First edition, 2019

Published by TOYO PRess
Visit us at: **www.toyopress.com**

Copyright © 2019 by William de Lange

The moral right of the author has been asserted.

All rights reserved. No part of this publication may be reproduced, stored or introduced into a retrieval system, or transmitted, in any form or by any means (electronic, mechanical, photo-copying, recording or otherwise), without the prior written permission of both the copyright owner and the above publisher of this book.

ISBN: 978-94-92722-164

Preface

To any student of the Japanese language, the staggering number of their onomatopoeia seems so daunting that one simply does not know where to begin. What on earth, for instance, is the difference between からから, かりかり, くりくり or こりこり. They may sound pretty similar to the foreign ear, but to the trained Japanese ear they carry a wealth of information, modulated by emphasis, context, and grammatical function. Thus からから can be used to describe someone laughing loudly, a vehicle rattling along, being parched with thirst, or being out of money. かりかり might have fewer usages, and though it sounds pretty similar, it has the distinctly different meanings of being crispy, or being irritable. The same is true for くりくり, which is used to describe either something fat and rotund, or round and lovable. Only こりこり carries a similar meaning (to かりかり) of being crunchy, but then more chewy.

Japanese onomatopoeia number in the thousands. They are, as in any living language, also in constant flux. One glance into any Japanese *manga* comic makes it clear that new onomatopoeia are coined almost on a daily basis. Others, which no longer seem to fit today's use, tend to fade into obscurity, only to be found in texts or recordings sometimes no older than a few decades.

Not surprising, then, that many a foreign speaker of the Japanese language prefers to fall back on the old and trusted verb-noun combination, with a few idioms thrown in for good measure. Japanese onomatopoeia seem just too obscure, too much tied to the inscrutable Japanese psyche to really grasp, let alone study in depth. Most perniciously, they are often frowned upon by Western academia (the product of a indo-European tradition that—except for early childhood—happens to rely less on onomatopoeia to express human experience. It seems that to the Wester ear, especially the 'educated' ear, onomatopoeia are somehow regarded as less important, less worthy of serious attention—a perception unjustly justified by their predominance in *manga*.

It is probably for all the above reasons that Japanese onomatopoeia are being paid so little attention by the (academic) institutions that are supposed to help the foreign student master the Japanese language. Nor do some of the dictionaries do a very good job. Except for a limited number of adverbial forms such as *chotto* or *yukkuri* the vast number of Japanese onomatopoeia fail to make their way into the syllabuses and dictionaries for foreign learners. They are considered an afterthought, a secondary aspect of the language, to be mastered as one slowly finds one's way into the more idiomatic areas of a language.

Preface

Consequently, it is usually only those who have lived and worked in Japan over many years who are able to master this to a Japanese far more natural and familiar vernacular. In doing so they are far more in tune with Japanese of all walks of life. Indeed, the native Japanese speaker does not perceive a clear distinction between onomatopoeia and the more formal expressions. Hip youths in the bars and clubs of Roppongi converse in a language rich with onomatopoeia derived from Japan's rich pop culture. At the same time, within the walls of Japan's universities, erudite academics sprinkle their lectures with onomatopoeia, and even the most respected of newspapers will employ onomatopoeia to describe the gravest of economic conditions, be they sluggish (のろのろ) or booming (ぐんぐん)–the English equivalent itself arguably an ideophone.

It is for this very reason that it is so crucial for the foreign student to get to grips with this rich and fascinating aspect of especially the Japanese language as early as possible. Together with Japanese idioms and proverbs, onomatopoeia make up a vast area of the Japanese language that is obscured in many textbooks, yet are used on a daily basis in all areas of Japanese life and culture. The earlier one develops a feel for Japan's vast pallet of onomatopoeia, the closer one will get to a side of the Japanese language that is in touch with 'real' Japanese.

CATEGORIES

Though often grouped together for convenience as onomatopoeia (as in the title of this dictionary and in the introduction above) Japanese ideophones, as they are collectively known, can be broken down into two distinct categories: onomatopoeia and mimetic expressions. Onomatopoeia are expressions that imitate real sound, be they human, animal voices, or otherwise. Mimetic expressions, by contrast, 'mimic' abstract notions: they describe the sound humans (in this case the Japanese) have come to associate with a certain emotion, a certain movement, or a certain state of things.

The Japanese distinguish five main categories into which their ideophones can be broken up. They are:

Giseigo (擬声語) sounds made by animals and humans (onomatopoeic)
Giongo (擬音語) sounds made by inanimate objects and nature (onomatopoeic)
Gitaigo (擬態語) sounds describing a condition or state (mimetic)
Giyōgo (擬容語) sounds describing movement and motion (mimetic)
Gijōgo (擬情語) sounds describing feelings (mimetic)

Preface

Of these five, the first two are most prevalent in the English language. Far fewer are the latter three. They are the mimetic expressions: they mime the condition, movement, or feeling described. It is their sparsity in Western languages that make Japanese mimetic expressions so hard to grasp to Western students.

TRANSLATING JAPANESE IDEOPHONES

Though the English language is not wholly devoid of mimetic expressions, thier occurrences are few and far between. Nor are they always readily apparent. Obvious mimetic expressions are compounds like dilly-dally, nitty-gritty, or wishy-washy. But less obvious words like glow and glimmer also have a clear association with light in the minds of English speakers. Equally, the words dawdle, fiddle and diddle, convey a hesitancy of movement that goes deeper than just their meaning. And in the same way that smash and crash call up a certain sound in the listener's ear, words like slosh and slush are instinctively associated with wetness.

Professional translators, whose job it is to convey the subtle nuances of a language, find it hard to convey the many onomatopoeia they find on their way while tackling a Japanese text. A study by Hiroko Inose clearly shows how much the Western reader of Japanese translations misses out on. In her study she extracts the number of onomatopoeia and mimetic expressions from the Japanese novel *Sputnik no koibito* (1999) by Haruki Murakami, and their number in the English and Spanish translations. Her findings are revealing. The original work contains 267 mimetic and 28 onomatopoeic expressions. The Englsih translation, by contrast, only contains 53 mimetic and 4 onomatopoeic expressions; while the Spanish translation carries only 49 mimetic and 8 onomatopoeic expressions.

This is not to say that the translators are at fault. Given the sparsity of English ideophonic expressions, there simply is no way to convey each and every expression with an English equivalent. Consider a poem by Shuntarō Tanigawa:

あなたは大げさねと女は言う
あの人はボソボソ話しただけよ
ペラペラしゃべったりはしなかったは
いやむしろガミガミ喚いていたよ
ブツブツと男は言う
あなたみたいにウジウジ言うのより良いは
サバサバと女は答える

Preface

In the whole poem, consisting of 14 verses, the poet uses 10 onomatopoeia and mimetic expressions. Compared to that, the loss of ideophonic expressions is clearly on display in the English translation:

> 'You exaggerate, don't you,' the woman says.
> 'She just snapped at me!
> Not glib or anything like that;
> no, she just yelled at me,'
> the man mutters.
> 'Better than being wishy-washy like you,'
> the woman replies airily.

The only clear English ideophonic equivalent in this one verse is the mimetic expression 'wishy-washy' (as a substitute for ウジウジ), though 'snapped', and 'mutter' might qualify. Given the limited ideophonic vocabulary in English and other (Indo-) European languages, the translator is forced to resort to other grammatical means to convey the meaning and 'feel' of the original by using adverbs, adjectives, verbs, nouns, phrasal verbs, idioms, or a combination of the above.

PREDICTABILITY OF IDEOPHONES

In spite of the bewildering multitude of Japanese ideophonic expressions, there is one great advantage they have over all other words: they are not arbitrary. What does this mean? Contrary to first impressions, the assignment of ideophonic expressions for any given sound, feeling, movement, or state, is somehow linked to a linguistic mechanism that seems to be universal—even across languages.

This phenomenon is most obvious in onomatopoeia. Despite regional differences, most languages will have similar expressions to describe a mooing cow, a barking dog, or a meowing cat—no language lets a lion squeak, a mouse roar.

But even in the case of mimetic expressions, i.e., expressions that describe a certain emotion, physical state, or movement, there seems to be a remarkable linguistic mechanism at work. In his groundbreaking research into onomatopoeia and mimetic expressions, the British academic Gwilym Lockwood finds that:

> There seem to be universal tendencies for people to associate certain sounds with certain meanings, regardless of language background. The vast majority of people link large vowels like *a* to large objects, small vowels like *i* to small objects, voiceless consonants like *k* to fast objects,

Preface

and voiced consonants like g to slow objects. This tendency is especially pronounced in ideophones, a special class of words which depict sensory information like sight, touch, movement, and sound. This means that people can accurately guess the meanings of Japanese ideophones, even if they don't speak Japanese at all, because of this iconic relationship between sound and meaning.

He drives home his point by presenting the following list of Japanese mimetic expressions that at first sight seem totally alien and incomprehensible. However, if one carefully weighs the words in one's mouth one will find that, even though one might not be familiar to their use, one is able to determine their general meaning when forced to decide between two opposites:

nurunuru	dry or slimy?
pikapika	bright or dark?
wakuwaku	exited or bored?
iraira	happy or angry?
guzuguzu	moving quickly or slowly?

Most people instinctively choose the correct answer (slimy, bright, exited, angry, and slowly). This, according to Lockwood, shows that there is something about ideophones that somehow corresponds to the way in which onomatopoeia have evolved, i.e., there is a corelation between the actual sound of the expression and the perceived condition. This phenomenon is therefore also referred to as sound symbolism: the sound symbolizes what we intuitively perceive to be the nature of the emotion, state or movement we seek to describe. In contrast to regular words, which tell us what something is, ideophones are words that describe things in a way that is close to our emotions. As a result they have a very powerful expressive quality. Though Lockwood does not go so far to say so, they probably come closest to the kind of language spoken by antediluvian man.

KEYS TO UNDERSTANDING JAPANESE IDEOPHONES

There are other, more concrete, ways one can find one's way into ideophonic language. Especially in Japanese, there are a large number of ways in which the foreign student can find her/his way into this bewildering maze of apparently similar or unrelated sounding onomatopoetic and mimetic expressions. To understand this we need to look at the Japanese alphabet.

Preface

Unlike in English, the Japanese alphabet is largely phonetic—that is, each sound is spelled in the same way it is pronounced. It is also extremely regular in that it consists of forty-six basic characters, most of which consist of a consonant-vowel combination: *ka, ki, ku, ke, ko; ta chi, tsu, te, to*, etc. These, to a Japanese ear, *pure* sounds (静音せいおん) become *unpure* (濁音だくおん) when they are voiced: *ga, gi, gu, ge, go*. In writing this is done by adding the symbol ゛, the so-called *dakuten* (also *tenten*), or by adding the symbol ゜, the so-called *handakuten* (also called *maru*). Thus the pure syllable か (*ka*) becomes the impure syllable が (*ga*), and the pure syllable は (*ha*) become the impure ば (*ba*) and ぱ (*pa*).

All this is relevant because the voicing of Japanese consonants is an important aid to understanding mimetic expressions. For one, the impure (voiced) sounds always feel louder. Thus the mimetic expression *gongon* is used for 'banging,' while the pure (unvoiced) expression *konkon* is used for knocking. Similarly, the expression *dondon* is used for 'drumming,' while the pure (unvoiced) expression *tonton* is used for tapping.

The choice of vowel can be an indication of a mimetic expression's meaning, for vowels, too, have a distinct feel to them. The vowels あ, う and お suggest something that is long, languishing, slow. Thus the vowel あ suggest the continuous downpour of rain in 雨あめがざあざあ降ふる. Likewise, the vowel い suggests something that is quick, nimble, or small, as in 金をちびちびと使う, 'use one's money sparingly.' The vowel え often has a negative ring to it, as in へらへらとした態度, 'a flippant attitude.'

The ending of an expression can be another important indicator. As in the first example above, the occurrence of the vowels あ, う and お at the end usually suggests a sound or action that is continuous or protracted. Ending an expression with a glottal stop, by contrast, suggests that—like the sound itself—something comes to an abrupt end. In writing the glottal stop is represented by a small っ. Given the purpose of the expression they often consist of just one (voiced) syllable, as in げっ 'to gag on *sth*,' or かっ 'to cough *sth* up.' They are also often followed by the particle と, as in ぱっと emphasizing a 'sudden' or 'swift' action. Another frequent ending is in り, which often conveys a sense that something is complete, rounded, definitive. Here, too, a small っ is often used for emphasis. Thus ぴったり is be used to convey the sense that an action has come to a definitive end, as in 彼女かのじょは煙草たばこをぴったり止とめた, 'she gave up smoking altogether.' Similarly, かっちり is used to describe a tight and exact fit. Expressions ending with ん, finally, convey a sense of something reverberating, spreading out unhindered in all directions, like a resounding temple bell (ぼーんと鳴なった寺鐘てちがね).

Preface

Reduplication, too, is often an important indicator to an ideophone's meaning, as it can suggest a repetition of sound, action, or number. Obvious examples are the many onomatopoeia that reduplicate syllables to suggest sound repetition: わんわん 'woof-woof', にゃんにゃん 'meow-meow,' があがあ 'quack-quack.' In mimetic expressions reduplication is often used to the same effect. Thus ごろごろ clearly suggests to repetitive rumbling of a thunder storm, while がたがた is evocative of the constant clatter of a loose mudguard on a cobbled road. The same is true for character compounds. Thus 時時 is used to indicate that something is repeated in time, or done regularly. Or it can be used to indicate multiple numbers, as in 人人. In such cases the iteration mark 々 saves having to write the character twice, so just 時々 and 人々.

KANJI-DERIVED IDEOPHONES

Not all entries listed in this dictionary are strictly speaking onomatopoeia or mimetic expressions. Though they are often written in *hiragana*, as already indicated above, a large number of mimetic-like expressions derive their meaning from (a repetition of) Chinese *kanji*, as in いろいろ [色々], つぎつぎ [次々], and もともと [元々]. It is for this reason that the *kanji* origins of these pseudo-onomatopoeia is provided in brackets for all relevant entries.

Because of their origin, *kanji*-derived expressions behave grammatically differently from regular onomatopoeia or mimetic expressions. Many of them, like だんだん [段々], can take the optional と. Some, like どうどう [堂々], only occur with と. Still others, like べつべつ [別々], only occur with に or の.

Some expressions, like あつあつ [熱々] or うきうき [浮き浮き], might seem *kanji*-derived, but are actually made by doubling the adjective (熱い) or verb (浮く) stem forms. Their grammatical behavior is closer to genuine ideophones, though they never have と or り endings.

GRAMMATICAL FUNCTIONS

Japanese onomatopoeia and mimetic expressions are used in a variety of grammatical ways. As evinced by the example of Murakami's novel, the most common use is that of an adverb. In such cases they can occur with or without the particle と or sometimes に, though in some cases the particle is required. Added more frequently in written than spoken Japanese, the particle helps to emphasize the aural quality of the expression and to prevent word order confusion.

Preface

A second important way in which (only) mimetic expressions are used is as an adjective. To achieve this the Japanese add した or だ, so the expression can modify a noun, as in あっさりとした味 (an uncomplicated taste). These are the formal ways. Less formal ways are by adding している, as in いそいそしている (be in high spirits), or the even more colloquially してる.

Adjectival mimetic expressions can also take on a noun-like grammar. To achieve this the Japanese add の, as in ばらばらの髪 (loose hair), な, or になる as in ばらばら〜になる (break up; become scattered).

The final way in which Japanese mimetic expressions can be used is as a verb unit. To achieve this the Japanese simply add the all-purpose する, as in どきどきする (be exited), or its less formal form やる.

Having said that, the sample sentences given in this dictionary are self-explanatory, and should suffice to bear out the different meanings, nuances, and contexts in which the ideophones are used. The grammatical markers are merely meant to show the different grammatical structures in which the expressions can occur:

- [Av] As an adverb modifying regular verbs or *kanji* compounds with する.
- [Aj] As an adjective modifying a noun with した or している (coll. してる) or だ.
- [N] As an adjective with noun-like grammar with な, の or になる.
- [する] As a verb unit combined with the all-purpose する or やる.

HIRAGANA OR *KATAKANA*

Generally, Japanese onomatopoeia and mimetic expressions can be written either with *hiragana* or *katakana*. As a (vague) general rule, onomatopoeia are written with *katakana*, while mimetic expressions are written with *hiragana*, though this rule is not always strictly observed. For emphasis, an author can also choose to write mimetic expressions with *katakana*, which lends it more *punch*. The rough equivalent is the use of *italics* in English and other European languages.

One notable though rare exception to this rule are the ideophones that derived from foreign languages. Thus ジグザグ, which is derived from the English mimetic expression 'zig-zag,' is always written with *katakana*. As is チックタック, which is derived from the English onomatopoeia 'tic-tac.'

The other exception are, as already mentioned above, the expressions that derive from Chinese. They can be written in three ways: with their original *kanji*, with *hiragana*, or (for emphasis) with *katakana*.

Preface

A final thing to keep in mind is that when written with *hiragana*, the long vowel 'u' can be written either with the character う or with the symbol ー, as in ぐーぐー (snoring), which could therefore also be written as ぐうぐう. Here, for the sake of consistency and ease of use, entries are (with the exception of loanwords) written with *hiragana*, and all long vowels are written with the symbol ー, as they would when the expression is written with *katakana*.

CROSS-REFERENCES

Cross-references are marked by a red arrow (▶) and placed at the end of entries. They are meant to guide the user to similar or related expressions, and do not indicate synonymous expressions. For the sake of clarity, no cross-references are given for successive entries with a similar meaning or nuance.

In addition, tags have been added to help the foreign learner distinguish between expressions that are archaic, idiomatic, dialect, elegant, colloquial, vulgar, or slang. These tags can be found in the main entries, as well as the Japanese and English sample sentences:

Main entries:	Sub-entries	Sample phrases
Ⓐ archaic	ⓐ archaic	ⓘ idiomatic equivalent
Ⓗ historic	ⓘ idiom	Ⓐ abstract equivalent
Ⓓ dialect	ⓓ dialect	Ⓛ literal equivalent
Ⓔ elegant	ⓔ elegant	Ⓔ elegant equivalent
Ⓒ colloquial	ⓒ colloquial	Ⓒ colloquial equivalent
Ⓥ vulgar	ⓥ vulgar	Ⓥ vulgar equivalent
Ⓢ slang	ⓢ slang	Ⓢ slang equivalent

あ

あーん open wide; wailing
- 〔Av〕子供が〜と泣き出した the child began to wail.

あいあい [藹々] 〔E〕〔A〕harmonious
- 〔N〕ⒺⒶ 〜たる ❶ peaceful; harmonious. ❷ luxuriant; verdant.

あおあお [青々] 〔E〕green; verdant
- 〔Av〕Ⓔ 〜(と)茂る grow lush.
- 〔Aj〕Ⓔ 〜(と)した海原 the emerald sea.

あかあか [赤々] bright red; bright
- 〔Av〕夕日が〜(と)照り映えた the setting sun set the sky on fire.

あかあか [明々] brightly lit; lit up
- 〔Av〕各窓が電灯〜(と)輝いていた every window was ablaze with electric light.
- ◆ めいめい

あぐあぐ gnawing; munching
- 〔Av〕犬が〜(と)骨を噛んだ the dog eagerly gnawed on the bone. ガムを〜噛み締める munch on a piece of chewing gum.
- ◆ がじがじ ◆ くちゃくちゃ

あくせく [齷齪] fussily; busily
- 〔Av〕毎日〜と働く ⓒ work like a dog every day.
- 〔する〕〜する fuss over sth; get worked up.
- ◆ こせこせ

あせあせ 〔G〕flustered; panicky
- 〔Av〕ⓒ 〜と手を振る wave one's arms in panic.
- 〔Aj〕ⓒ 〜とした準備 last-minute preparations.
- ◆ あたふた

あたふた hurriedly; hastily
- 〔Av〕〜と部屋を出る leave the room in a hurry.
- 〔する〕〜する hurry.
- ◆ あせあせ

あっけらかん 〔G〕blankly; vacantly
- 〔Av〕ⓢ 〜と眺める stare vacantly at sth.
- 〔Aj〕ⓢ 〜としている be indifferent.
- ◆ ぼそっ

あっさり easily; lightly; quickly
- 〔Av〕〜(と)不倫を認める readily acknowledge one's infidelity. 〜(と)断る reject sth out of hand; flatly refuse sth. 〜(と)やめる give up without a fight.
- 〔Aj〕〜とした味つけ lightly seasoned. 〜とした味 an uncomplicated taste.

い

〜とした食事 a light meal. 〜とした人 an easy-going person.

♦ さっぱり ♦ すっきり

あっぷあっぷ floundering

[A] 〜ともがく be about to drown.
[A] 不景気で〜している struggle to make ends meet due to a recession.

あぶあぶ gurgling; frothing

[A] ⓐ 泉の水が〜と浮き上がった water gurgled up from the spring. 赤ちゃんが〜(と)寝ていた the baby mumbled in its sleep.

♦ こぼこぼ

ありあり clearly; vividly

[A] 悲しさが彼女の顔に〜(と)見える the sorrow is clearly visible on her face. 〜(と)目に浮かぶ have a vivid recollection (of *sth*). 〜(と)見える see *sth* clearly/vividly.

♦ くっきり ♦ はっきり ♦ まざまざ

あんぐり open-mouthed

[A] 〜(と)口を開けて見とれる look on in amazement; stare at *sth* in disbelief.

あんあん [暗々] gloomy

[A] ⓔⓐ 〜(と)した森 a gloomy forest.

♦ うつうつ [鬱々]

い

いがいが thorny; sharp

[A] 〜した海胆 a thorny sea urchin.

♦ とげとげ

いきいき lively; vividly

[A] 〜(と)描写する give a vivid description. 〜(と)働く work with relish.
[A] 〜(と)した表情 an animated expression. 〜(と)した想像力 a vivid imagination. 〜(と)した通り a bustling street. 〜(と)した生活を送る lead an active life.
[す] 〜する be lively; be active.

いざこざ trouble; difficulties

[N] 〜の種 the seed of trouble. 〜を起こす cause trouble. 〜を避ける avoid trouble.

♦ ごたごた ♦ どさくさ ♦ ごちゃごちゃ

いじいじ hesitantly; timidly

[A] 〜(と)悩む ⓒ dilly-dally on *sth*.
[A] ⓢ 〜した奴 ⓒ a wishy-washy character. ⓢ 〜とした野郎 ⓥ a spineless dude. 〜した声 a faltering voice.
[す] 〜する hesitate; ⓒ dilly-dally.

♦ おずおず ♦ うじうじ ♦ おどおど

いそいそ cheerfully; excitedly

Av ～(と)出かける leave in good spirits.

Aj ～している be in high spirits; be elated.

♦ わくわく

いちゃいちゃ ⑤ flirt; make out

する ⑤ ～する dally (with a girl); flirt. ⑤ ～するカップル a flirtatious couple. ⑤ 彼氏と～する ⓒ make out with one's boyfriend.

いらいら [苛々] ⑥ irritation

する ⓒ ～する become irritated; lose patience; ⓥ ⑤ be pissed off. ⓒ ～させる irritate sb; ⓘ rub sb the wrong way; ⓘ get on sb's nerves.

♦ じりじり ♦ むしゃくしゃ

いんいん [殷々] ⓔ roaring

Av ⓒ ～(と)響く roar; thunder.
N ⓒ ～たる砲声 the roar of guns.

う

うおーん howl; aooo

Av ～と遠吠えする狼 howling wolves.

うかうか carelessly; negligently

Av ～(と)騙される be cheated as a result of one's negligence; ⓒ be conned into sth. ～(と)秘密を漏らす give away a secret negligently; ⓘ spill the beans inadvertently.

する ～する be negligent; be careless; ⓘ let down one's guard. ～するな pay attention! ⓒ look sharp!

♦ うっかり ♦ ぼやぼや

うきうき cheerfully; buoyantly

Av ～と旅に出かける set off on a journey in high spirits.

Aj ～している be in high spirits.

する 心が～する feel elated; ⓘ be on cloud nine.

うごうご wriggle; writhe

Av 大量の幼虫が～と這い出した a large number of larva crawled out. ～と蠢く邪悪 creepy evil spirits.

うざうざ in swarms; tedious

Av ⓐ ～(と)蠢く crawl along. ⓐ ～文句を言うな stop whining; stop complaining.

Aj ⓐ 毛虫が～している the caterpillar crawled/wriggles along.

する ⓐ ～する swarm with (insects).

♦ うじゃうじゃ ♦ うようよ ♦ ぞろぞろ

うじうじ hesitantly; irresolutely

Av ～(と)考え込んでしまう become irresolute; brood over sth.

Aj ～した性格 be indecisive; ⓒ be wishy-washy.

ウジウジ

する ～する be irresolute.

♦ いじいじ ♦ おずおず ♦ おどおど

うじゃうじゃ in swarms; tedious

Av ～(と)蠢く crawl along. ～言う whine about *sth*; go on (and on) about *sth*. 子供が～いる have loads of children; have a large family.

Aj 毛虫が～している the caterpillar crawled/wriggled along.

♦ うざうざ ♦ うようよ ♦ ぞろぞろ

うずうず eagerly; impatiently

Av ～言う mutter; grumble. 虫歯が夜通しに～(と)痛んだ the bad tooth ached all night.

Aj ～している be eager to do *sth*; ⓘ champ at the bit.

♦ ぶつぶつ ♦ むずむず

うぞうぞ Aj be (sexually) aroused

Av ⓐ ～誘う be (sexually) aroused.

うだうだ B long-winded; boring

Av ⓑ ～言う be long-winded. ⓒ ～言われている ⓒ be driven to distraction.

うつうつ [鬱々] E gloomily

Av ⓒ ～(と)茂る grow lush.

する ⓒ ～する be downhearted; be dejected; be despondent.

♦ あんあん [暗々]

ウットリ

うっかり carelessly; inadvertently

Av ～(と)忘れてしまう forget all about *sth*; let *sth* totally slip one's mind. ～(と)秘密を漏らす give away a secret negligently; ⓘ spill the beans inadvertently. ～(と)乗り越す miss one's stop; fail to get off on time. ～(と)ぶつかる meet by accident; ⓒ bump into each other.

♦ うかうか

うっすら lightly, faintly; slightly

Av ～と覚える remember *sth* faintly. ～(と)記憶に残っている have a dim recollection of *sth*. ～と目を開ける open one's eyes slightly. ～(と)陰りを差す cast a faint shadow (over *sth*).

♦ ほんのり

うっすり thinly; lightly; slightly

Av ～と目を開ける open one's eyes slightly. ～(と)化粧する put on light makeup.

うっとり spellbound; ecstatic

Av ～(と)聞き惚れる listen in rapture. 新車を～(と)眺める admire a new car.

する ～する be ecstatic; ⓘ be on cloud nine; ⓒ ⓘ be blown away. ～する美人 a breathtaking beauty.

♦ ぼーっ ♦ ぽかん

ウツラウツラ / ウンウン

うつらうつら drowsily; vividly
- Ⓐ ～と眠る doze off; nod off.
- Ⓢ ～する be drowsy; nod off.
- ♦ まざまざ

うとうと dozing; nodding off
- Ⓐ ～と眠る doze off; nod off.
- Ⓢ ～する doze off; nod off.
- ♦ こくこく ♦ こくりこくり ♦ こっくり

うねうね winding; meandering
- Ⓐ ～(と)連なる山並み a winding mountain range. 永遠に～(と)折れる山道 an endlessly winding and folding mountain road.
- Ⓐ ～とした川筋 a meandering river.
- ♦ くねくね ♦ ジグザグ

うはうは 俗 exhilarated; all smiles
- Ⓐ ◎宝くじが当たって～だ be over the moon with winning the lottery.
- Ⓢ ◎株が上がって～する be delighted with the rising stocks.

うまうま successfully; completely
- Ⓐ ～(と)話に乗る fall for sb's story; be taken in by sb's story. ～と一杯を食わされる be completely taken in; be fooled; fall into sb's trap.

うようよ crawling with; in swarms
- Ⓐ 貧乏が～(と)この世にいる the world is awash with the poor.
- Ⓐ 毛虫が～している the caterpillar crawled/wriggled along.
- ♦ うざうざ ♦ うじゃうじゃ ♦ ぞろぞろ

うらうら gently; softly
- Ⓐ 日は～と家の屋根を照らした the sun played gently on the roofs of the houses. 夕日は～と川面に映った the setting sun played over the surface of the river.
- Ⓐ ～とした春の光 the gently rays of spring.
- ♦ やんわり

うるうる teary-eyed; moist
- Ⓐ ～した瞳 eyes filled with tears.
- Ⓢ ～する be in tears.

うろうろ loiteringly; restlessly
- Ⓐ ～(と)出口を探す aimlessly look for the exit.
- Ⓢ 道に迷って～する be lost; lose one's way. ～するばかりだ be in a state of shock; be stunned.
- ♦ おたおた ♦ まごまご

うろちょろ loiteringly
- Ⓐ ～(と)歩き回る walk around aimlessly.
- Ⓢ ～する loiter about; hang around.

うんうん groaning; grunting
- Ⓐ 痛くて～(と)唸る groan with

pain. 彼らは〜（と）相槌を打った they chimed in with grunts of approval.

うんざり tedious; boring; fed up

[する] 〜する be fed up with *sth*; be bored.

♦ けんなり

え

えいえい [営々] hard; ardently

[Av] 〜と働く work hard; work strenuously.

えっちらおっちら laboriously

[Av] 〜（と）坂を登って行く climb the slope with great difficulty.

えへらえへら sniggle; chuckle

[Av] 彼は何時も〜（と）笑っている he is always sniggling (at nothing).

えんえん [延々] E forever; eternally

[Av] 会議は〜（と）一昼夜に及んだ the meeting dragged on for a whole day and night.

えんえん [奄々] E gasping; panting

[Av] E 気息〜としている be gasping for breath.

♦ ぜいぜい ♦ はーはー ♦ ふーふー

えんえん [炎々] E blazing

[Av] E 〜と燃え盛る火事 a blazing fire.

えんえん [蜿々] E meandering

[Av] E 〜と流れている川 a meandering river.

お

おいおい boohoo; waaa

[Av] 〜（と）泣く cry one's heart out.

おうおう [往々] E occasionally

[Av] E 〜にして生じる arise occasionally. E 〜にしてある事だ be common; happen from time to time.

おうおう [怏々] E melancholily

[する] E 〜とする be melancholic; be dejected; be downcast.

おぎゃあ wailing; mewling

[Av] 赤ん坊は〜（と）泣く the baby wails. 〜（と）泣く子猫 mewling kittens.

おっとり boohoo; waaa

[Av] 〜（と）泣く cry one's heart out.

おずおず timidly; nervously

[Av] 〜（と）頭を下げる timidly hang

one's head. 〜(と)手を差し伸べる timidly extend one's hand. 〜(と)微笑する smile timidly. 彼女を〜(と)目で追った his eyes nervously followed the girl. 時雨が〜(と)偲び寄った the autumn shower hesitantly crept closer.

[する] 〜する tremble (with fear); be apprehensive; be intimidated.

♦ いじいじ ♦ うじうじ ♦ おどおど

おたおた speechless; shocked

[する] 〜する be in a state; be shocked.

♦ うろうろ ♦ まごまご

おっとり quietly; gently; calmly

[Av] 〜(と)構える be composed; be graceful.

[Aj] 上品で〜した人 a refined and graceful person.

おどおど hesitantly; coweringly

[Aj] 〜とした目付き a timid look.

[する] 人前で〜する be shy in front of people. 〜して口籠る stammer nervously. 〜してしまう get flustered; ⓒ lose one's cool.

♦ いじいじ ♦ うじうじ ♦ おずおず

おめおめ shamelessly; brazenly

[Av] 良くも〜(と)私の前に姿を表したね you have some check to show up here! 今さら〜(と)帰れない can't possibly go back after this. 彼らは〜(と)敵に後ろを見せた they shamefully retreated. 〜(と)屈服する suffer a humiliating defeat. 〜(と)諦める give up without a fight.

おろおろ nervously; flustered

[Av] 彼女が〜(と)泣いた she wept in chocking sobs.

[Aj] 〜した声 a faltering voice.

[する] 〜してしまい get flustered; be at a loss.

おんおん bawling; crying

[Av] 〜(と)泣く weep bitterly; ⓒ cry one's eyes out.

おんおん [温々] [E][A] quiet; calm

[Aj] ⓒⓐ 〜(と)した部屋 a comfortable room. ⓒⓐ 〜(と)した性質 (have) a calm temperament.

♦ ぬくぬく

か

がーがー quack; croak; gabble

[Av] 鴨が〜鳴った the duck quacked. 蛙が〜鳴った the frog croaked. スピーカーが〜言っている the speaker is making a lot of noise. 〜言わないでくれ stop nagging at me!

かいかい / ガサッ

かいかい [恢々] E wide; spacious
N ⓔⓐ 〜たる vast; spacious.
♦ばくばく [漠々] ♦まんまん [漫々]

がいがい [皚々] E A white; silver
N ⓔⓐ 〜たる山 snow-clad mountains.

かくかく [赫々] E brilliant; glorious
N ⓔ 〜たる熱帯地方の太陽 the brilliant sun of the tropics. ⓐ 〜たる戦果を収める make great military gains.

がくがく wobbly; loose
A 脚が〜(と)震える have one's knees give way.
する 〜する wobble; be loose. 歯が〜する have a loose tooth.
♦ぐらぐら ♦ふらふら

がくがく [諤々] E A outspoken
N ⓐⓔ 〜たる outspoken; straightforward; candid.

がくん suddenly; jerkingly
A 運動した時首が〜となりました my neck snapped during exercise. 〜と膝をつく feel one's knees give way; sink to one's knees 成績が〜と落ちた my grades suddenly dropped. 電車が〜と動き出した the train lurched into motion. 地下鉄が〜と止まった the subway stopped with a jolt. 温度が〜と下がった the temperature suddenly dropped.
♦がっくり ♦がらり ♦がばっ

かさかさ dry; bone-dry; rustling
A 〜(と)落ち葉を踏んで歩く walk while the fallen leaves crunch underfoot. 〜(と)音を立てる rustle; make a rustling sound.
A 〜した肌 dry skin.
N 〜になる become dry. 〜のパン dry bread.

がさがさ dry; rough; rustling
A 〜(と)音がする rustle; make a rustling sound. 藪を〜(と)分けて進む move through the rustling bushes.
A 〜した肌 rough skin; chapped skin. 〜した人 an unpolished person; a crude person; a course character.
N 〜になる become chapped. 〜の手 a chapped hand.

かさこそ rustling; swishing
A 〜(と)舞う落ち葉 rustling leaves.

がさごそ rustling; scurrying
A 鼠が〜(と)走り回っている the mice are scurrying around.
♦ごそごそ

がさっ swoosh; swoop; plunge
A 積もった雪が〜と落ちた the

ガサッ　　　　　　　　　　　　　カタカタ

piled-up snow came down in a swoosh. 仕事が〜と減った the number of jobs plunged.

がしがし roughly; briskly; loudly
[Av] 地下深くまで〜(と)掘り進める dig deep into the ground. 〜(と)初稿を作る make a rough first draft. ◎ 母は息子の頭を〜(と)撫でた the mother tousled the hair of her son's head. 〜(と)活動する学生達 students living a boisterous life. 〜(と)略図を描く make a rough sketch.

がじがじ biting; gnawing
[Av] 犬が〜(と)骨を噛んだ the dog eagerly gnawed on the bone.
[冭] 〜とする gnaw on *sth*.
◆ あぐあぐ ◆ くちゃくちゃ

がしっ firmly; solidly; heartily
[Av] 昔の友人が〜と抱き合った the old friends hugged heartily. 〜と相手を抑え込む hold *sb* down firmly.
[Aɪ] 〜とした造りの建物 a soundly built structure.
◆ がっしり

かしゃかしゃ clinking; rattling
[Av] 彼が算盤を〜(と)揺すった he shook the abacus (making it rattle).
[Aɪ] 〜(と)した音をする make a clinking noise.

がしゃがしゃ clinking; messy
[Av] 〜に散らかった部屋 a disorderly room. 〜(と)動く骸骨 a rattling skeleton. 袋〜に詰め込む stuff *sth* into a bag.

がじゃがじゃ messy; disorderly
[N] おもちゃ箱が〜になった the box with toys was in a mess. 〜の落書き messy graffiti.

かしゃっ clicking; snapping
[Av] 〜とシャッターを切る release the (camera) shutter with a snap.

がしゃっ cracking; crashing
[Av] 雨戸を〜と閉める close the shutters (of a house) with a crash.

かすかす dry; insipid; barely
[Av] 〜間に合う be just on time. 〜試験に通る squeak through an exam.
[Aɪ] 〜(と)した林檎 a dried-out apple.
[N] 葱が〜になった the scallions dried out.
◆ かつかつ ◆ ぎりぎり ◆ すれすれ

かたかた clattering; rattling
[Av] 〜(と)下駄を鳴らして歩く walk on noisy *geta*. 〜言う音 a rattling sound.
◆ かちゃかちゃ ◆ からから ◆ からり

9

がたがた rattling; whining

[Av] 〜(と)震える tremble with fear. 〜言うな ⓒ stop whining!
[Aj] 蓋が〜だ the lid fits poorly. 〜している be poorly organized
[する] 〜する rattle/clatter/shake.

♦ がちゃがちゃ ♦ がらがら

かたこと clattering; rattling

[Av] 台所で〜(と)音がする there is a clattering (sound) in the kitchen.

がたごと clattering; rattling

[Av] 貨車が〜(と)止まった the freight train ground to a rattling halt.

がたっ clunking; clanking; slump

[Av] 人気が〜と落ちた (her) popularity suddenly dropped. 列車が〜と動き出した the train started with a clank. 〜と揺れが来た (we) felt a sudden tremor.

がたぴし rattling; creaking

[Av] 扉が〜(と)いう the door creaks.
[する] 〜する creak/rattle. 会社の経営が〜(と)する the company's management is creaking (with internal tensions).

♦ きしきし ♦ ぎちぎち ♦ みしみし

がたん bump, bang, crash

[Av] 売り上げが〜と落ちた profits came crashing down. 椅子が〜と倒れた the chair fell over with a crash.

♦ だーん ♦ どかん ♦ どん

かちかち ticking; knocking; hard

[Av] 火打石を〜(と)鳴らす/打つ strike a flint (to make fire). 時計が〜(と)動いている the clock is ticking. 歯が〜(と)鳴る one's teeth chatter (with cold).
[Aj] 〜だ be rigid (in one's thinking); be obstinate.
[N] 〜になる ❶ become hard. ❷ freeze up (with nerves); ⓒ be scared stiff. 〜のパン hard bread.

♦ こちこち ♦ かちんかちん

がちがち rigidly; chattering

[Av] 歯を〜(と)言わせる make one's teeth chatter (with cold). 〜(と)凍る freeze solid; freeze up.
[Aj] 〜だ be rigid (in one's thinking); be obstinate.
[N] 〜になる ❶ become hard. ❷ freeze up (with nerves). 〜の勉強家 an over-diligent student.

♦ こちこち

かちっ click; clank; plock

[Av] 二人の目が〜と合った their eyes locked on to each other. 〜とスイッチを入れる flick on a switch. 〜と固定する click sth in place.

内容の〜とした本 a book with a tight plot.

がちっ clank; wham
彼が泥棒を〜と抑え込んだ he held the thief down firmly.
〜とした知識を積み重ねる accumulate a thorough knowledge.

かちゃかちゃ clattering; clanging
〜(と)皿を重ねる noisily pile up the dishes. 〜(と)鍵を回す音 the clinking sound of a turning key.
♦ かたかた ♦ からから

がちゃがちゃ clinking; rattling
〜(と)食器を洗う noisily wash the dishes. 〜(と)文句を言う noisily complain. 〜(と)鳴る轡虫 the rattling song of a Japanese bush cricket.
〜になる be in a mess; get into a tangle; ⓔ be in a state of confusion.
♦ かたかた ♦ がらがら ♦ からり

がちゃっ crashing; cracking
皿が〜と二つに割れた plate broke in two with a crack.

がちゃり clanking; clinging
手錠が〜とかかる lock the handcuffs with a clank.

がちゃん slamming; crashing
〜と窓ガラスが割れた the window broke with a crash. 〜と電話を切る slam the phone down.

かちり click; clack
〜と電気をつける switch on the light/electrical appliance. 〜と鍵を回す turn the key with a click.

かちん clinking; clanging
グラスを〜と触れ合わせる touch glasses. シャッターを〜と押す press the (camera) shutter. 戸の掛け金を〜と掛ける latch a door; close the latch on a door. ⓢ 〜と来る be annoyed; ⓘ be rubbed the wrong way; ⓥ ⓢ be pissed off.

かちんかちん hard; unyielding
〜に凍る freeze solid; freeze up. 〜に冷却する freeze sth hard. 〜に乾く dry sth hard. 〜に固くなる grow as hard as stone; become stone-hard.
〜だ be rigid (in one's thinking); be obstinate.
〜に固くなる grow as hard as stone; become stone-hard. 〜の石頭だ be hard-headed.
♦ かちかち ♦ こちこち

かっ suddenly; resolutely

A 〜と目を見開く open one's eyes wide. 空が〜と晴れてきた the sky suddenly cleared. 太陽が〜と照りつけた the sun beat down (on the savannah).

N ⑤ 〜となる ⓪① hit the ceiling. ⓪ blow one's top. ⑤① go ballistic; Ⓥ⑤ be pissed off.

♦ かんかん

かっか hotly; briskly; fiercely

A 火が〜と燃える the fire burns briskly. ⑤ 頭に〜と来る be angered; ① be rubbed the wrong way; Ⓥ⑤ be pissed off. 頭が〜と火照る grow red in the face; get flustered. 〜と照りつける太陽 the scorching sun.

する 〜とする ❶ burn hotly; burn briskly. ❷ be angered; be upset; ⓒ lose one's cool.

かつかつ [戛々] clicking; clacking

A 革の靴音が〜廊下に響いた the sound of leather shoes echoed down the hallway.

N ⓒ 〜たる下駄 clip-clopping geta.

♦ かすかす ♦ ぎりぎり ♦ すれすれ

かつかつ ⑤ barely; narrowly

A 荷物が〜に届いた the parcel arrived just in time. ⑤ 〜間に合う be just on time.

A ⑤ 〜だ be barely enough; scrape by.

N ⑤ 〜の生活をする eke out a living; ① scrape along.

♦ かすかす ♦ ぎりぎり ♦ すれすれ

がつがつ ⑤ greedily; covetously

A ⑤ 〜(と)食う eat greedily; ⓒ eat like a pig.

する ⑤ 〜する be greedy; covet sth.

がっかり disappointed; exhausted

する 〜する ❶ be exhausted; feel (emotionally) drained. ❷ be dejected; be disappointed; be disheartened.

♦ げっそり ♦ げんなり

がっくり dejected; crestfallen

A 〜(と)首を垂れる drop one's head (in disappointment). 〜(と)肩を落とす drop one's shoulders (in disappointment). 〜(と)膝をつく feel one's knees give way; sink to one's knees. 客足が〜(と)減った (the shop) lost a lost a lot of customers.

する 〜する be dejected; be heartbroken; feel crushed.

♦ がくん ♦ がらり ♦ がばっ

がっくん dejected; disappointed

A 首を〜と垂れる drop one's head

(in disappointment). 〜と肩を落とす drop one's shoulders (in disappointment).

がっしり firmly; solidly; tough

[Av] 〜（と）組み合わせる put *sth* firmly together; make a solid assembly. 〜（と）固定する fasten *sth* tightly. [Aj] 〜（と）した構え a firm stance. 〜（と）した上半身 a muscular torso. 〜（と）した体格 a strong (physical) build.

♦ がしっ

がったん clunk; clank

[Av] 列車が〜と動き出した the train started with a shudder.

かっちり tightly; exactly

[Av] 計画が〜（と）立てる make a tightly fitting plan. ネジを〜（と）掴む get a tight grip on a screw. [Aj] 〜（と）した体格の男 a man with a strong build/physique.

♦ きっかり ♦ ぴったり

がっちり tightly; exactly; shrewd

[Av] 〜（と）区別する make an exact distinction. 〜と仕上がる give *sth* a tight/exact finish. 〜（と）手を握る grip *sb*'s hands tightly. 〜（と）金を貯める save up money steadily. [Aj] 〜（と）した服装 a tight-fitting dress. 〜（と）した印象 a trim/chic impression. 〜（と）した男 ❶ a hard-headed man; ⓒⓘ a hard-boiled guy. ❷ a stingy fellow; a tight-fisted guy. ❸ a shrewd man; a smart guy.

♦ きっちり ♦ しっかり

かっちんかっちん hard; knocking

[Av] 〜に凍る freeze solid; freeze up. 〜と石を刻む chip away at a stone. [N] 〜に固くなる grow as hard as stone; become stone-hard.

♦ こちこち ♦ かちんかちん

がっぷり tightly; firmly

[Av] 力士は〜（と）四つに組んだ the *sumō* wrestlers locked squarely with each other.

がっぽがっぽ in large quantities

[Av] 金を〜（と）稼ぐ earn vast sums of money. 〜（と）儲かる make huge sums of money; ⓘ make money hand over fist; ⓒⓘ rake it in. 焼きそばを〜（と）食い捲る work one's way through huge quantities of *yakisoba*. 〜（と）金を貯める accrue vast amounts of money.

がっぽり in large quantities

[Av] 〜（と）儲かる make huge sums of money; ⓒⓘ rake it in. 〜（と）金を貯める accrue vast amounts of money.

ガツン／ガヤガヤ

がつん klunk; whonk; thump

- Av ～と言ってやる give sb a good talking to. ～と顎に一発かます give sb a good wallop on the chin.
- ♦ ごつん ♦ ごん ♦ どかっ ♦ どっか

がばがば gushing; gulping; baggy

- Av 水が～(と)水槽に入り込んだ the water gushed into the water tank. ～(と)儲かる make huge sums of money; Ⓒ ① rake it in. ⓥ 飯を～(と)貪り食う devour one's food; Ⓒ gabble sth up.
- Aj コートが～だ be coat is oversized.
- N ～のジャンパ a baggy jacket.
- ♦ がぶがぶ ♦ ぐいぐい ♦ ごくごく

がばっ suddenly; quickly

- Av ～と起き上がる get up suddenly; rise suddenly.
- ♦ がくん ♦ がっくり ♦ がっ

がびがび dried stiff; parched

- N スープを零したシャツが～になった the shirt onto which I had spilled the soup became stiff (when dried).
- ♦ ごわごわ

がぶがぶ gulping; guzzling

- Av ～(と)ビールを飲む gulp down beer; drink beer in one gulp.
- Aj ビールで腹が～だ feel the beer slosh around in one's stomach.
- ♦ がぶがぶ ♦ ぐいぐい ♦ ごくごく

がぶり biting; chewing; gulping

- Av 酒を～(と)飲み込む down the sake in one gulp. 犬が肉に～(と)食いついた the dog snatched the piece of meat. 痩せ犬が狩人の腕に～(と)噛み付いた the wild dog sank its teeth into the hunter's arm.

がぼがぼ gurgling; squelching

- Av ～(と)音を立てる make a gurgling sound. ～(と)湧き出る温泉 a spluttering onsen. ～(と)泡を立てる spew forth lathers of foam.

がみがみ nagging; snarling

- Av ～言う nag sb; snap at sb. ～(と)叱りつける scold sb severely; ① give sb a dressing-down.
- ♦ やいやい

がやがや noisily; clamor

- Av つまらない事に～(と)騒ぎ立てる make a fuss over a trifling matter. 大勢の人が～(と)集まってきた a large crowd had gathered in a clamor. ～(と)論じる have a noisy discussion.
- Aj 居酒屋が～とした雰囲気だった a noisy atmosphere filled the izakaya.
- する 教室の中が～(と)していた the

ガヤガヤ　　　　　　　　　　　　　ガラリ

classroom was in a state of uproar.
- ざわざわ ● わいわい ● わーわー

からから dried-up; parched
[Av] ～(と)笑う laugh loudly (with glee); burst into laughter; laugh cheerfully. ～(と)下駄の音を立てる make one's *geta* clapper (over the pavement). 馬車が～(と)動いた the horse-drawn cart rattled along.
[Aj] 喉が～だ be thirsty; ⓒ be parched with thirst. 財布が～だ be out of money; be penniless; ⓒ ⓘ be broke.
[N] ～になっている be dried up; become parched.
- げたげた ● けらけら ● ころころ

がらがら rattling; clattering
[Av] 馬車が～(と)止まった the horse-drawn cart came to a rambling stop. ～(と)嗽をする gargle noisily. 岩が～(と)崩れ落ちた the rocks crumbled with a clattering noise. ～(に)痩せた子供達 emaciated children. 彼は～(と)血を吐いた he threw up blood. 壁が～(と)倒れた the wall came crumbling down.
[Aj] 初発電車は～だ the first train was almost empty.
[N] 風邪で声が～になった have a hoarse voice because of a cold.
- がたがた ● ごろごろ

からころ clattering; clip-clop
[Av] 下駄を～(と)いわせて道を通る clip-clop along the street.
- からんころん

がらっ burst (open); suddenly
[Av] 扉が～と開ける throw open the door. 外観を～と変える give *sth* a whole new face. 彼女の世界観が～と変わった her world view changed dramatically/was upset. 性格を～と変える ⓒ ⓘ change one's spots.

からり clattering; cheerfully
[Av] 箸が～と床に落ちた the chopsticks fell clattering to the floor. 障子を～と開ける slam open the *shōji*. 空が～と晴れ上がった the sky cleared up. ～と忘れてしまう forget all about *sth*; completely slip one's mind. ～と笑う laugh cheerfully.
[Aj] ～とした性格を持つ be open-minded; have a frank disposition.
- かたかた ● かちゃかちゃ ● からり

がらり fully; suddenly; rudely
[Av] 雰囲気が～と変わった the mood suddenly changed. 彼が～と変わった he has changed completely. 扉を～と開ける fling the door open. 石垣が～と崩れた the stone wall crumbled with a crash.
- がくん ● がっくり ● がばっ

ガラン　　　　　　　　　　　　　　　　　　　　ガンガン

がらん empty; deserted
- Av 石油缶が〜と倒れた the oil can fell over with a clang.
- Aj 〜とした体育館 an empty gym.

からんからん clanging; pealing
- Av 鐘が〜と鳴った the bell made a hollow peal.
- ♦ こーん ♦ ごんごん

からんころん clapper; clip-clop
- Av 彼は〜（と）下駄を鳴らした he clip-clopped on his *geta*.
- ♦ からころ

かりかり crisp; grumpily
- Av 煎餅〜（と）音を立てて噛む munch on a rice cracker.
- Aj 〜している ❶ be crispy. ❷ be on edge; be irritable. 〜（と）した菓子 a crunchy sweet. 〜（と）したベーコン crisp bacon.
- N 〜になる become crispy.
- ♦ こりこり ♦ ぽりぽり

がりがり skinny; crunchy
- Av 〜（と）勉強する study feverishly. 窓を〜（と）引っ掻く scratch against the window. 〜に痩せている be emaciated; ⓒ ⓘ be skin over bones.

がん thump; thud; difficult
- Av 〜と鳴る make a dull sound. 脳天を〜と撃つ give a heavy blow to the crown of *sb*'s head. ⓢ と一発〜と言ってやる ⓒ ⓘ give *sb* a good dressing down. 〜という目に合わせる make *sb* pay (for *sth*).

かんかん clanging; blazing; furious
- Av 土が〜に凍る the earth is frozen stone-hard. 刀鍛冶が鋼を〜（と）鍛えた the swordsmith hammered the steel.
- Aj 〜（と）している真夏の日 the scorching summer sun.
- N ⓢ 〜になる become irate; be seething (with rage).
- ♦ かっ

かんかん [閑々] composure
- Aj 〜としている be composed.

がんがん pounding; intense
- Av 耳が〜（と）鳴る have a buzz-ring in one's ear(s). ラジオを〜（と）鳴らす play a radio at full blast. 〜（と）稽古する practice relentlessly; go at one's practice hammer and tongs.
- する 頭が〜する have a throbbing headache; ⓒ have a splitting headache.
- ♦ じんじん ♦ ずきずき ♦ ずきん

き

きーきー squeaking; screeching

[Av] 子供が母の耳元に〜(と)喚いた the child screeched in its mother's ear. 油が切れて軸受けは〜(と)鳴った having run out of oil the bearing squeaked awfully.

ぎーぎー creak; rasp

[Av] ぶらんこを〜(と)漕ぐ swing oneself on a screeching swing.

きーん pinging; zinging; tzinging

[Av] 〜と耳鳴りがする hear a shrill ringing in one's ear. 〜と冷えた冬の朝 a piercing cold winter morning.

ぎくしゃく jerky; stilted; stiff

[Av] 〜(と)椅子から立ち上がる stand up stiffly from one's chair.
[Aj] 〜した空気 an uncomfortable atmosphere. 夫婦の間が〜している relations between the couple are strained. 〜した物腰 awkward movements. 〜した歩き方 a jerky way of walking. 〜した言い方 a stilted way of talking. 〜したお辞儀 an awkward bow.

ぎくっ startled; suddenly

[Av] 〜と腰に痛みが走った there was a sudden pain in my hip.
[する] 〜とする be startled/shocked.
♦ ぎょっ

ぎくり startling; shocking

[する] 〜とする be startled/shocked.
♦ ぎっくり ♦ びっくり

ぎこぎこ squeaking; creaking

[Av] 〜(と)板を曳く saw away on a board. 櫂を〜(と)引く pull the creaking paddles.

ぎざぎざ jagged; notched; milled

[N] 〜のかど a jagged edge. 〜になった縁 a (postcard's) serrated margin; a (coin's) milled edge.

きしきし squeaking; creaking

[Av] 床板が〜(と)鳴った the floor boards creaked.
♦ がたぴし ♦ ぎちぎち ♦ みしみし

ぎしぎし squeaking; aching

[Av] 〜(と)踏み板を鳴らす cause the footboards to squeak. 戸が〜(と)軋んだ the door creaked on its hinges. 鞄に服を〜に詰め込む stuff one's clothes into a bag. 身体中が〜(と)痛んだ my whole body ached.
[する] 〜(と)する ❶ squeak; creak. ❷ fail to go smoothly.

ぎすぎす stiff; strained; thin

[Aₗ] 〜した世の中 an inhospitable world. 〜（と）した体 an emaciated body. 〜（と）した態度 a stiff manner. 〜（と）した人間関係 strained relations.

きちきち grinding; jam-packed

[Av] 引き出しは〜（と）詰まっていた the drawers were jam-packed. 部屋代を〜（と）払う pay the rent for one's room to the last penny.

[N] 〜な靴 tight-fitting shoes.

ぎちぎち creaking; crammed

[Av] 柱が地震で〜（と）唸った the pillars groaned under the strain of the earthquake. 予定が〜（と）詰まっていた the schedule was crammed.

♦ ぎっしり ♦ ぎゅーぎゅー ♦ びっしり

きちん neatly; precisely; tidily

[Av] 家賃を〜と払う pay the ful rent exactly on time. 〜と定刻に着く be exactly on time. 〜と食事する have the right table manners.

[Aₗ] 〜とした neat; tidy. 〜とした生活を送る lead an orderly life.

[する] 〜とする tidy sth up.

きっかり exactly; precisely

[Av] 一時〜に始める start at exactly one o'clock. 山の稜線が〜と見える the mountain ridge is clearly visible. 〜と予言する predict sth exactly.

[Aₗ] 〜とした計算 a precise calculation. 〜とした角度 an exact angle.

♦ かっちり ♦ ぴったり

ぎっくり startling; shocking

[Av] ⓒ 〜（と）睨む glare/stare.

[する] 〜（と）する be startled/shocked.

♦ ぎくり ♦ びっくり

ぎっしり tightly; crammed

[Av] 〜（と）書かれた手紙 a closely written letter. 店が〜（と）並んでいた the shops stood close together. 予定は〜だ the schedule is tight.

♦ ぎゅーぎゅー ♦ びっしり

ぎっちら creaking; squeaking

[Av] 〜（と）舟を漕ぐ row a boat with a creak of the oars.

きっちり precisely; punctually

[Av] 戸を〜（と）閉める close the door tightly. 〜（と）理解する understand sth precisely. 朝食で〜（と）栄養を摂る strictly guard one's nutritional intake for breakfast.

♦ がっちり ♦ しっかり

ぎっちり ◎ tightly; crammed

[Av] ⓒ 〜（と）詰まっている be closely packed.

ギッチリ　　　　　　　　　　キューキュー

[A] ⓪ 家は〜だった the house was closely packed.
♦ぎっしり ♦ぎゅーぎゅー ♦びっしり

きっぱり clearly; plainly; flatly
[Av] 〜（と）断る flatly refuse (to do sth). 〜（と）物言う be to the point; ⓪ call a spade a spade.
[AJ] 〜（と）した立場を示す take a clear stance. 〜（と）した謝罪 a clear admission of guilt. 〜（と）した返事 a definitive answer.
♦すっぱり ♦はっきり

ぎとぎと oily; greasy; sticky
[AJ] 〜とした食べ物 greasy food. 〜とした手 sticky hands.
[する] 〜する be oily/greasy.

きびきび briskly; lively
[Av] 〜と歩く walk lively; keep up a brisk pace. 〜と動く move vigorously. 〜と働く work energetically.
[AJ] 〜（と）した文書 a vigorous writing style. 〜（と）した体操 vigorous exercise. 〜（と）した店員 an energetic shop assistant.
♦てきぱき ♦すたすた ♦ばきばき

きゃーきゃー squeal; shriek
[Av] 猿が〜（と）鳴いた the monkey shrieked. 子供達が〜（と）笑っていた the children squealed with laughter.

ぎゃーぎゃー screech; scream
[Av] 野党が〜（と）反対していた ⓒⓘ the opposition screamed bloody murder. 〜（と）喚くな stop making such a fuss!

きゃっきゃっ chitter; chatter
[Av] 〜と燥ぐ子供達 the cackle of children making merry. 猿が〜と大騒ぎをした the monkey made a din of a noise.

きゃふん dumbstruck; speechless
[Av] 〜と言わされた be argued down; ⓒⓘ be beaten hollow.

きゃんきゃん yelping; yapping
[Av] 〜（と）吠える子犬 a yelping puppy.

ぎゃんぎゃん yelling; whining
[Av] 耳元で〜（と）喚く yell in sb's ear.

きゅーきゅー squeaking; tightly
[AJ] 新しい靴が〜（と）鳴る the new shoes squeaked. 帯を〜に閉め上げる pull the obi tight. 財布が〜言っている money is tight; ⓒⓘ live on a shoestring. 仕事で〜言っている be buried under a pile of work.
[A] 金が〜（と）している money is tight; ⓒⓘ live on a shoestring.

ぎゅーぎゅー creaking; tightly

- 革の椅子が〜いう the leather chair squeaks. 〜言わせてやる torment sb (with questions); ⓒ ① let sb have it. 縄で〜（と）縛る tighten sth with a rope until it creaks. 荷物を〜（と）詰める pack the luggage tight.
- 〜な目にあう run into trouble.

▶ ぎっしり ▶ びっしり

きゅーん ping; zing; tzing

- 機械は〜と音を立てた the machine was whining. 胸が〜となった be overwhelmed (with emotion).

きゅっ tightly; in one sweep

- 髪の毛を〜と縛る fasten one's hair tightly. 〜と口を詰む purse one's lips. ガラスを〜と擦る scratch glass. 酒を〜と一杯飲む finish one's cup of sake in one gulp.

ぎゅっ tightly; firmly; hard

- タオルを〜と絞る wring a towel. 手を〜と握る squeeze sb's hand. 〜と掴む hold sth tightly.

ぎゅんぎゅん droning; humming

- 〜という工事現場の音 the noise of a construction site. ヘリが〜と飛んだ the helicopter hummed.

▶ ぶんぶん

ぎょっ startled; suddenly

- 〜と驚く be startled.
- 〜とする be startled/shocked.

▶ ぎくっ

きょときょと nervous; restless

- 〜（と）辺りを見回す look around anxiously.
- 〜（と）した目付き a frightened look.
- 〜する be fidgety; be nervous; be on tenterhooks.

きょとん blankly; staring

- 〜（と）びっくりする be utterly amazed; be totally bewildered.
- 〜（と）した顔をして with a blank look; with a look of amazement. 〜（と）した表情をする wear a blank look of utter amazement.
- 〜とする be nonplussed; be bewildered.

きょろきょろ restlessly; nervously

- 〜（と）辺りを見回す look around restlessly.
- 〜する let one's eyes wander; be inattentive. 〜するな pay attention!

▶ けろけろ

ぎょろぎょろ goggling; rolling

- 〜（と）目を回す roll one's eyes. 〜（と）辺りを睨み回す look around

with prying eyes. 痩せた老人の目が～と眼窩から～突き出した the emaciated old man's eyes protruded from their sockets.
- [Aj] ～していた/とした目 with goggling eyes.
- ♦ ぐりぐり

きらきら sparkling; glittering
- [Av] 星が～(と)輝く the stars twinkled. 子供の目に涙が～(と)光った tears glistened in the child's eyes.
- [Aj] ～(と)した瞳 glimmering pupils.
- [する] ～する sparkle; glitter.

ぎらぎら glaring; dazzling
- [Av] ～と光り輝く真夏の太陽 the blazing summer sun.
- [Aj] ～していた/とした目 with glaring eyes.
- [する] ～する glare; glimmer.
- ♦ けいけい

きらり sparkling; glistening
- [Av] 涙が彼女の目に～(と)光った tears glistened (momentarily) in her eyes.

ぎらり glistening; glimmering
- [Av] 侍は大刀を～(と)抜き放った the samurai drew his sword with a flash. 男の目が～(と)光った the man's eyes glimmered ominously.

きりきり tightly; grinding; briskly
- [Av] 弓を～(と)引き絞る pull a bow taught. 腹が～(と)痛む have a terrible stomach pain. ～(と)回る spin around wildly. 紐を～と縛り上げる fasten a rope tightly. ～(と)立ち働く work hard; ① stay on the grind.
- [Aj] 日程は～だ the schedule is overly crammed. 汚染の許容量～だ pollution levels have reached the limits (of what is permissible).

ぎりぎり barely; grinding
- [Av] ～(と)歯を食い縛る grind one's teeth. 紐で～と縛る bind sth tight with a rope. ～で間に合う be only just in time; barely make it.
- [Aj] 利益が～だ only just make a profit.
- ♦ かすかす ♦ かつかつ ♦ すれすれ

きりり tightly; tensely; creaking
- [Av] 口を～(と)結ぶ purse one's lips. 帯を～(と)締める tightly fasten an *obi*. 弓を～(と)引き絞る pull a bow taught. ～(と)鳴る櫂 a creaking oar.
- [Aj] ～(と)した顔立ち a tense expression.

きろきろ restlessly; nervously
- [Av] ⓐ 辺りを～(と)睨め回す look around restlessly.

きんきらきん gaudy; showy; flashy
- Av ～に飾り立てる dress up in fancy clothes; ⓒ ① deck oneself out.

きんきん shrill; piercing; cold
- Av ～に冷やしたビール ice-cold beer.
- Aj ～した子供の声 the high-pitched voice of children.

ぎんぎん harsh; grinding; ecstatic
- Av ～に踊りまくる dance with exilement. ～鳴く夏の蝉 the incessant roar of the summer cicadas.

く

くいくい tugging; moping; fretting
- Av ～(と)糸を引く tug at a string. ⓐ ～(と)悩む fret over *sth*; ⓒ mope over *sth*. ⓐ ～(と)腹が立つ fly into a sudden rage; ⓒ ① blow one's top. ⓢ ① go ballistic. ビールを～(と)飲んでしまう gulp one's beer down in a few swigs.
- ♦ くよくよ

ぐいぐい tugging; gulping
- Av ～(と)糸を引く tug hard at a string. 計画を～(と)推し進める push one's plan through. 腹が～(と)鳴る hear one's stomach rumble. ビールを～(と)飲んでしまう gulp one's beer down in a few swigs.
- ♦ がぶがぶ ♦ ぐびぐび ♦ ごくごく

ぐいっ suddenly; forcefully
- Av 綱を～と引っ張る give a rope a hard tug. 酒を～と飲み干す down (a cup of) sake in one gulp. ～と左に曲がる swerve to the left.
- ♦ ぐっ ♦ ぐん

ぐーぐー snoring; rumbling
- Av ～(と)高鼾をかく snore loudly. ① saw wood. お腹～がという have an empty/rumbling stomach. ～(と)眠り込む fall fast asleep.
- ♦ ぐっすり ♦ すやすや

ぐーすか sleep soundly/like a log
- Av ～寝ている be sound asleep; ⓒ ① sleep like a log.

くさくさ depressed; vexed
- する ～する ❶ feel depressed; ⓒ ① down in the dumps. ❷ be vexed; be on edge; be in a foul mood.
- ♦ むしゃくしゃ

ぐさぐさ thuck; tsak; piercing
- Av 革に～(と)穴を空ける cut a hole in the leather. 胸に～(と)突き刺さる pierce one's heart.
- N ～になる come undone; get scattered; become a mess.

ぐさっ thuck; tsak; hard-hitting

[A] 彼女の辛辣な一言が〜と胸にきた her caustic words pierced his heart; ⓒ her biting words hit home hard. 〜と胸にくる名言 a famous quote that deeply resonates. 〜と心に突き刺さる思い出 a heartrending recollection. 彼は刀を〜と足元に突き立てた he planted the sword next to his feet.

くしゃくしゃ crumpled; gloomy

[A] 手紙を〜(と)丸める crumple a letter into a ball. ガムを〜(と)噛む munch on a piece of chewing gum. 顔を〜(と)歪める wrinkle one's face up (with laughter/in agony).
[N] 〜になる become crumpled; get wrinkled. 〜な髪の毛 disheveled hair. 〜になったハンカチ a crumpled handkerchief. 〜の新聞 a crumpled (up) newspaper.
[する] 〜する be gloomy; be downcast. 顔を〜にする wrinkle one's face up (with laughter/in agony).

ぐしゃぐしゃ soggy; mushy; pulpy

[A] 段ボール箱を〜(と)踏み潰す crush the cardboard box (with one's feet). 〜(と)かき混ぜる mix (the ingredients) roughly together.
[Aj] 〜(と)した山道 a muddy mountain road.
[N] 車が正面衝突で〜になった the car was crushed by the head-on collision. 〜になったジャンパー a soggy jumper. タオルを水で〜にする soak a towel in water.

ぐしゃっ crushing; squashing

[A] 飛行機の模型を〜と踏み潰す crush the model airplane underfoot.

ぐしゃり squishing; squashing

[A] 蛙は車に〜と潰れた the frogs were squashed flat by the car.
♦ぺしゃり ♦ぺちゃんこ

くしゃん achoo; sneezing

[A] 彼女が〜と大きく嚔をした the woman sneezed loudly.

ぐしょぐしょ sopping; dripping

[A] 〜に濡れる be sopping wet.
♦びしょびしょ

くすくす chuckle; giggle; furtively

[A] 〜(と)笑い出す have a fit of giggles. 〜(と)笑っ giggle; chuckle. 陰で〜(と)笑う laugh in one's sleeve.
[Aj] 〜したやり方 a roundabout way (of doing things). 〜した笑い声 suppressed laughter; muffled laughter.
[する] ⓐ〜する be secretive; act secretively; be furtive.
♦くつくつ ♦へらへら

ぐすぐす sniffle; snuffle

- 風邪で鼻を〜(と)言わせる sniffle with a cold. 〜(と)鼻啜る sniffle.

♦ ぐつぐつ

ぐずぐず slowly; tardily; loose

- 〜と先延ばしにする put *sth* off; procrastinate. 〜と時を過ごす waste time; loaf one's time away. 〜文句を言う complain; grumble.
- 〜(と)した天気 unsettled weather.
- 〜になる come loose; come undone.
- 〜する drag one's feet. 〜するな step on it! look sharp!

♦ のそのそ ♦ のろのろ ♦ もたもた

ぐすん sniffle; snuffle

- 鼻を〜(と)鳴らす sniffle. 〜(と)啜り泣く声 the sound of sniffling sobs.

くたくた withered; tedious; mushy

- 〜に疲れる be exhausted; be done in; be knackered. 〜(と)煮える boil *sth* to pulp.
- もう〜だ be exhausted; be done in; be knackered.
- 〜になる become exhausted; grow tired. become mushy. become saggy; lose its shape. become threadbare.

♦ ぐったり ♦ へとへと

くだくだ tedious; lengthy; wordy

- 〜(と)述べ立てる give a long-winded speech. 〜(と)文句を言う make lengthy excuses.

♦ くどくど ♦ つべこべ

ぐだぐだ tedious; tiresome

- 〜(と)言い訳を続ける repeat the same excuse ad nauseam. 〜(と)暮らす lead a tiresome life. 〜言うな stop whining!

♦ くどくど ♦ つべこべ

くちゃくちゃ crumpling; messy

- 新聞を〜(と)丸める crumple up a newspaper. 〜(と)手紙を書き殴る dash off a messy letter. 〜(と)音を立ててガムを噛む munch noisily on a piece of chewing gum.

♦ あぐあぐ ♦ がじがじ

ぐちゃぐちゃ soppy; sloppy; pulpy

- 〜(と)文句を言う gripe about *sth*.
- 〜になる become messed up. become soggy; become sloppy; become pulpy. 〜の字 sloppy handwriting.
- 〜(と)した新聞 a soggy newspaper. 〜(と)した雪 pulpy snow. 〜(と)した御飯 gooey rice. 髪の毛が〜だ (my) hair is a mess. 部屋はいつも〜だ the room is always untidy.

グチャグチャ　　　　　　　　　　　　　　　　グッタリ

[する] 順番を〜にする mess up the order.

ぐっ suddenly; firmly; deeply

[Av] 綱を〜と引っ張る give a rope a hard tug. ビールを〜と飲み干す down one's beer in one gulp. 〜と目立つ stand out even more. 〜とくる make a deep impression. 〜と力を入れる put all one's strength into sth. 成績は〜と良くなった the results have increased dramatically.

♦ ぐいっ　♦ くん

くっきり distinctly; clearly

[Av] 〜(と)目立つ clearly stand out. 山の稜線が〜(と)見える the mountain ridge is clearly visible.
[Aj] 〜とした映像 a clear image.

♦ ありあり　♦ はっきり　♦ まざまざ

くっくっ cackle; coo; giggle

[Av] 鳩が〜と鳴る the pigeons coo. 堪えかねて〜と笑い出す (they) could not bear it any longer and burst out in suppressed laughter.

くつくつ stifled; simmering

[Av] 〜(と)笑い出す have a fit of giggles. 〜(と)笑う giggle; chuckle. 陰で〜(と)笑う laugh in one's sleeve.

♦ くすくす　♦ へらへら

ぐつぐつ boiling; simmering

[Av] 〜(と)音を立てる make a bubbling sound. 〜(と)煮込む simmer sth for a long time. 〜(と)鼻を言わせる sniffle.

♦ くすくす

ぐっしょり soaking wet; drenched

[Av] 〜(と)雨に濡れる be soaked with rain. 〜(と)汗を掻く sweat all over; Ⓔ perspire profusely.
[Aj] 〜だ be soaked; be drenched.

♦ びっしょり

ぐっすり sound; deep; wholly

[Av] 〜眠る be fast asleep; be sound asleep; Ⓒ Ⓘ sleep like a log. Ⓐ 財産を〜息子に譲る leave one's whole estate to one's son; pas one's etire fortune on to one's son. Ⓐ 片足を〜泥濘へ踏み込むる sink one foot deep into the mud.

♦ ぐーぐー　♦ すやすや

ぐったり exhausted; limp

[Av] 〜(と)横たわる lie down dead tired. 〜(と)力を抜く go completely limp. 〜(と)疲れる be exhausted; Ⓒ be done in; Ⓢ be knackered.
[する] 〜(と)する be exhausted; Ⓒ be done in; Ⓢ be knackered.

♦ くたくた　♦ へとへと

25

ぐでんぐでん dead drunk; pissed

- Av ～に酔っ払う be dead drunk; ⓒ ⓘ be plastered.
- N ～になる become blind drunk; ⓥ ⓢ get pissed.

♦ へべれけ ♦ べろべろ ♦ めろめろ

くどくど tedious; repetitive

- Av ～言うな stop whining! ～(と)不平を並べる keep on complaining; harp on about *sth*. ～(と)小言を言う keep lecturing *sb* on *sth*.

♦ くだくだ ♦ ぐだぐだ ♦ つべこべ

くにゃくにゃ soft; flexible

- Av ～(と)曲がった小道 a small and winding road. ～(と)曲げられる be flexible; be pliable.
- Aj ～(と)した食感 (have) a soft bite; (have) a soft texture.
- N ～になる ❶ become flexible; become pliable. ❷ become soft and cuddly.
- する ～(と)する ❶ be flexible; be pliable. ❷ be soft and cuddly.

♦ ふかふか

ぐにゃぐにゃ flabby; limp; pulpy

- Av ～(と)体をくねらせる contort one's body (into impossible shapes). ～(と)動くミミズ a wriggling worm. ～(と)道に倒れる collapse in the (middle of the road.

- Aj ～(と)した性格 (have) a weak character.
- N ～になる ❶ go limp; become flabby; lose shape. ❷ become pulpy; go mushy.
- する ～(と)する ❶ be flexible; be pliable. ❷ go weak-kneed; lose heart. ～するな pull yourself together!

♦ ふにゃふにゃ

ぐにゃり twisted; spineless; soft

- Av 根元が～と曲がった the roots were severely contorted.
- Aj ～としたものを踏みつける step into *sth* soft/mushy.
- Aj ～とした男 a spineless guy.

くねくね winding; twisting

- Av ～(と)曲がった山道 a winding mountain road. ～(と)曲がる川 a meandering river.
- Aj ～(と)した細道 a winding path.
- する 腰を～(と)させえて踊る dance with swaying hips.

♦ うねうね ♦ ジグザグ

ぐびぐび gulping; guzzling

- Av ～(と)飲む gulp *sth* down. 酒を～(と)やる ⓒ gulp down one's sake.

♦ がぶがぶ ♦ ごくごく ♦ ぐいぐい

ぐびりぐびり gulping; guzzling

- Av ～(と)大杯を干す gulp down a

large *sakazumi*.
♦ がぶがぶ ♦ ごくごく ♦ ぐいぐい

くやくや A worrying; fretting

[Av] 〜(と)待つ wait anxiously. 〜思う fret over *sth*; ⓒ mope over *sth*.

♦ くいくい

くゆくゆ A worrying; fretting

[Av] ⓐ 〜(と)待つ wait anxiously. ⓐ 〜思う fret over *sth*; ⓒ mope over *sth*.

♦ くいくい

くよくよ worrying; fretting

[Av] 〜思う fret over *sth*; ⓒ mope over *sth*. 〜(と)心配する worry about *sth*; agonize over *sth*.

[する] 〜するな stop fretting! ⓒ cheer up!

♦ くいくい

くらくら dizzy; giddy

[A] 頭が〜している my head is spinning.

[する] 〜する be dizzy; feel giddy.

♦ くらっ ♦ ふらっ ♦ ふらり

ぐらぐら wobbly; shaky; giddy

[Av] 大地が〜(と)来た the earth shook. 湯が〜(と)煮え立つ the water boils furiously. 〜(と)揺れる shake (vehemently). 〜(と)沸く boil away. 〜(と)頭が廻る feel one's head spinning. それは血が〜(と)煮え滾った it made my blood boil.

[する] 〜する ❶ be unsteady; be reeling; feel (very) shaky. ❷ be indecisive; waver; be irresolute. 歯が〜する have a loose tooth.

[N] 〜になる ❶ grow unsteady; come loose; feel (very) giddy; become wobbly. ❷ grow indecisive; start to waver; become irresolute.

♦ がくがく ♦ ふらふら

くらっ dizzy; giddy

[A] 〜とした feel dizzy; be giddy.

ぐらっ swaying; veering; lurching

[Av] 機体が〜と右に傾いた the fuselage suddenly lurched to the right. 船が〜と傾いた the ship suddenly listed. ビルが地震で〜と横揺れがした the building swayed from side to side due to the earthquake.

♦ くらくら ♦ ふらっ ♦ ふらり

くりくり big; round; rotund

[Av] 頭を〜に剃る shave one's head clean. 〜と太った人 a fat and rotund person.

[A] 〜した目 big round eyes.

ぐりぐり hard; grinding; rolling

[Av] 目を〜(と)回す roll one's eyes. 肩を〜(と)揉む massage *sb*'s shoulder.

くるくる whirling; rolling; spinning

〜(と)回す whirl around. 包帯を〜(と)巻く wind bandage (round a wounded limb). 〜(と)働く work hard; ① stay on the grind.

ぐるぐる curling; churning; coiling

〜(と)回ったような気がした I felt I was going round in circles. 〜(と)腕を振り回す wave one's arms around. 近所を〜(と)回る walk around the neighborhood. ターバンを〜(と)頭に巻き付ける wrap a turban around one's head. お腹が〜(と)鳴る my stomach is rumbling.

くれぐれ [呉々] repeatedly

〜頼む ask/implore sb repeatedly. 〜語る tell sth over and over again.

くわっ wide; gaping

〜と目を開く open one's eyes wide. 口を〜と開いて with gaping mouth; with one's mouth wide open.

ぐん firmly; greatly; noticeably

〜と押す give sth a hard shove. 綱を〜と引っ張る give a rope a hard tug. 品質は〜と落ちた the quality fell markedly.

♦ ぐいっ ♦ ぐっ

くんくん sniffing; whining

犬が地面を〜嗅いだ the dog sniffed the ground. 犬が〜鳴いた the dog whined.

ぐんぐん steadily; rapidly

〜飛ばせ step on it! 山道を〜(と)登る steadily climb the mountain road. 背が〜(と)伸びる grow steadily taller; keep on growing. 縄を〜引っ張る pull the rope with all one's might. 経済が〜(と)成長している the economy is booming.

♦ ずんずん

け

けいけい barking

〜と鳴く犬 a barking dog.

♦ けんけん

けいけい [軽々] indiscreetly

〜に判断する make an ill-conceived judgement.

けいけい [炯々] glaring; piercing

〜たる目 piercing eyes.

♦ ぎらぎら

けいけい [煢々] ⓔ solitude
- Ⓐ ⓒ ひと本の老杉が〜と立っていた the ancient cedar stood all by itself.

けーけー puking; retching
- Ⓐ 〜(と)吐く throw up.
- ♦ げろげろ

けたけた cackling; giggling
- Ⓐ 〜(と)笑う laugh foolishly; chuckle coquettishly; cackle; giggle.
- ♦ からから ♦ けらけら ♦ ころころ

げたげた boisterously; heartily
- Ⓐ 〜(と)笑う laugh loudly; give a horselaugh; roar with laughter (at a banal spectacle).
- ♦ からから ♦ げらげら ♦ ころころ

けちょんけちょん thorough; utter
- Ⓐ 〜にけなす run sb into the ground; ⓒ slam sb down. 〜にやっつける ⓢⓘ give sb hell.

げっそり ⓔ haggard; dejected
- Ⓐ ⓒ 〜(と)痩せる grow thin; become emaciated. ⓒ 頬が〜(と)痩ける have sunken cheeks. ⓒ 肉が〜(と)落ちる be emaciated; have gaunt features.
- Ⓢ ⓒ 〜する be dejected; feel downhearted.
- ♦ がっかり ♦ げんなり

けばけば gaudy; garish; loud
- Ⓐ 〜した be gaudy; be garish.

げほげほ coughing; choking
- Ⓐ 〜(と)咳込む have a fit of coughing. 〜(と)咳をする have a wet cough. 〜(と)煙に噎せる choke on the smoke.
- ♦ ごほごほ ♦ ごほん ♦ こんこん

けらけら cackle; chuckle; giggle
- Ⓐ 〜(と)笑う laugh foolishly; chuckle coquettishly; cackle (with mirth); giggle (with enjoyment).
- ♦ からから ♦ げたげた ♦ ころころ

げらげら guffawing; haw-hawing
- Ⓐ 〜(と)笑う give a horse laugh; laugh heartily.
- ♦ からから ♦ げたげた ♦ ころころ

けろけろ croaking; nervously
- Ⓐ 〜(と)鳴っている蛙 croaking frogs. 〜(と)辺りを見回す look around restlessly.
- ♦ きょろきょろ

げろげろ ⓢ retching; barfing
- Ⓐ ⓒ 〜(と)吐く throw up. ⓢ 〜(と)鳴っている蛙 croaking frogs.
- Ⓢ ⓒ 〜する retch; barf; puke.
- ♦ けーけー

けろり entirely; nonchalantly

- Ⓐ ～(と)約束(やくそく)を忘(わす)れてしまう forget all about one's appointment. 頭痛(ずつう)(と)治(なお)った the headache lifted completely. 嵐(あらし)の空(そら)が～(と)晴(は)れた the stormy skies cleared up completely.
- Ⓐ ～(と)した顔(かお)をする look unperturbed. ～している be indifferent about sth; be unperturbed by sth. ～(と)した態度(たいど)をとる Ⓒ take sth in one's stride.

けんけん hopping; barking

- Ⓐ 狐(きつね)が～(と)鳴(な)く a fox barks.
- Ⓐ ～(と)した言葉(ことば) cutting remarks; harsh words.
- する ～する hop on one foot.

♦ けいけい

げんなり Ⓒ dejected; wearily

- する Ⓒ ～(と)する ❶ be exhausted; feel (emotionally) drained. ❷ be dejected; be disappointed; be disheartened. ❸ be exasperated; Ⓒ be fed up.

♦ うんざり ♦ げっそり

こ

こうこう [煌々] Ⓔ brilliantly

- Ⓐ Ⓒ ～とした電灯(でんとう) a brilliant light.

♦ さんさん [燦々] ♦ さんらん [燦爛]

ごうごう [轟々] rumbling

- Ⓐ 列車(れっしゃ)が～と鉄橋(てっきょう)を渡(わた)った the train thundered across the railway bridge. 滝(たき)が～と音(おと)を立(た)てた the waterfall thundered (past).

♦ ごろごろ

ごーん gong; bong; zunk; zong

- Ⓐ 鐘(かね)が～(と)鳴(な)った the bell made a hollow peal.

♦ からんからん ♦ ごんごん

こくこく dozing; gulping

- Ⓐ ～と居眠(いねむ)りをする doze off; nod off. 焼酎(しょうちゅう)を～(と)飲(の)み下(くだ)す gulp down one's *shōchū*.

♦ うとうと ♦ こくりこくり ♦ こっくり

ごくごく gulping; chugging

- Ⓐ ～(と)ワインを飲(の)む gulp down one's wine.

♦ がぶがぶ ♦ ぐいぐい ♦ ぐびぐび

ごくり gulping; chugging

- Ⓐ ～(と)ワインを飲(の)み下(くだ)す gulp down one's wine.

♦ ぐびぐび ♦ ごくごく

こくりこくり dozing; nodding off

- Ⓐ ～と居眠(いねむ)りをする doze of; nod off. ～と頷(うなず)く nod (in agreement).

♦ うとうと ♦ こくこく ♦ こっくり

ごくん gulping; chugging
- A ～とワインを飲み下す gulp down one's wine. ～と薬を飲み込む drink one's medicine in one gulp.
- ◆ ぐびぐび ◆ ごくごく ◆ くくり

ごしごし scrubbing; rasping
- A 床を～(と)擦って洗う scrub the floor hard.
- Aj ～(と)した部屋 a cluttered room; a messy room.

ごしゃごしゃ jumbled; messy
- N 彼女の髪が～になった her hair was in disarray.
- ◆ ごみごみ

こせこせ fussy; fidgety; cramped
- A ～(と)動き回る fidget about.
- Aj ～(と)した庭 a cramped garden.
- する ～する make a fuss.
- ◆ あくせく

こそこそ sneakily; furtively
- A ～(と)行動する act suspiciously. ～(と)携帯を見ている secretly look at one's (smart)phone. ～(と)出て行く sneak out (of a place).
- ◆ こっそり ◆ ひっそり

ごそごそ rustling; rummaging
- A 押し入れを～(と)探し回る rummage through a closet.

- する ～する rustle; make a noise.
- ◆ がさごそ

ごそっ completely; entirely
- A 品物を～と盗まれた have all one's things stolen. 会員が～と減ってしまった the number of members had dropped dramatically.

ごたごた discord; mess; muddle
- A 野菜を～(と)煮込む boil vegetables together. ～(と)混ざっている be mixed up; ⓒ be thrown together. ～言うな stop grumbling!
- Aj ～(と)した町 a disorderly town.
- N ～を起こす cause trouble.
- する ～する be in a mess; get into a tangle; ⓒ be in a state of confusion.
- ◆ いざこざ ◆ どさくさ ◆ ごちゃごちゃ

こちこち ticking; knocking; hard
- A 岩を～(と)削る whittle away at a rock. 時計が～(と)時を刻む the clock counts the hours. 火打石を～(と)鳴らす/打つ strike a flit (to make fire).
- Aj ～だ be rigid (in one's thinking); be obstinate.
- N ～になる ❶ become hard. ❷ grow tense; become nervous. ～の餅 a hard rice cake.
- ◆ かちかち

ごちゃごちゃ jumble; mix up

- ～(と)混ざっている be mixed up; ⓒ be thrown together. あれこれを～(と)考える mix (different) things up in one's mind. ～言うな stop grumbling!
- ～(と)している be in a mess; ⓒ be in a state of confusion. ～(と)した話 an incoherent story.
- ～になる be in a mess; get into a tangle; ⓒ be in a state of confusion.
- ～にする confuse things; mix things up.

♦ いざこざ ♦ ごたごた ♦ どさくさ

こちょこちょ coochy-coo; tickling

- ～(と)擽る tickle a child. ～(と)耳打ちする whisper closely into *sb's* ear. ～(と)動き回る bustle about busily.

ごちょごちょ grumbling; whining

- いつまでも～(と)言うな stop whining all the time.

こちんこちん hard; tense

- 土が～に凍る the earth is frozen stone-hard.
- 入学試験で～(と)になる be nervous for one's entrance examination.

こっくり nodding; dozing; subdued

- ～と頷く nod one's head (in approval). ～と居眠りをする doze off; nod off.
- ～した紺色のスーツ a subdued navy-blue suit. ～した煮出し stock with a subdued flavor.
- ～する doze off; nod off.

♦ うとうと ♦ こくこく ♦ こくりこくり

こつこつ tapping; steadily

- ドアを～(と)叩く knock on the door. 靴音が～廊下に響いた the sound of leather shoes echoed down the hallway. 毎日～(と)続く日記 faithfully keep a day-by-day diary. ～(と)苦労を重ねる toil laboriously; ⓘ stay on the grind; ⓢ slug away.

♦ せっせ

ごつごつ rugged; scraggy

- ～(と)した岩 a rugged rock. ～とした人 an unpolished person; a crude person; a course character.

こっそり stealthily; secretly

- 部屋を～(と)忍び込む furtively enter a room. 裏口から～(と)抜け出す escape secretly through the rear entrance.

♦ こそこそ ♦ ひっそり

ごっそり completely; entirely

- 宝石が～(と)盗まれた all the jewels were stolen. 毛が～(と)抜け

る lose all one's hair; lose all its hair; lose its coat. 壁が〜(と)崩れた the wall had completely collapsed.

こってり thickly; richly; strong

🅰 〜(と)化粧すり apply heavy makeup. 〜(と)◎油を絞る take sb to task; ◎ tell sb off; ◎ haul sb over the coals.
🄰 〜(と)した料理 rich food. 〜(と)した口当たり a strong taste.
◆でこでこ

こっとんこっとん thump; thud

🅰 水車が〜と回る the waterwheel is treading water.

こつん bonk; plock; tock

🅰 木の実が〜と窓に当たった the nut fell against the window with a plonk. いたずらがばれて、彼は父親に〜とやられた being found out, he was rapped over the head by his father.

ごつん thud; thump; bang

🅰 〜と壁にぶつける bump into a wall. ◎ 〜と来る take a blow; be hit hard; hit home hard.
◆がつん ◆ごん ◆どかっ ◆どっか

こてこて ⓒ thickly; richly

🅰 ◎ペンキを〜(と)塗り重ねる apply many layers of paint. ◎ 白粉を〜(と)塗る apply a thick layer of face powder. ◎ ジャムを〜(と)塗り付ける put on a thick layer of jam.
🄰 ◎〜(と)した飾り付け gaudy decorations.

ごてごて ⓒ thickly; gaudy

🅰 ◎〜(と)不平を並べる pour forth one's complaints thick and fast; voice one complaint after the other. ◎〜(と)飾り立てる decorate sth lavishly. ◎自我が〜言う talk incessantly about oneself; be full of oneself.
🄰 ◎〜(と)した飾り付け gaudy decorations. ◎〜(と)した味付け rick seasoning.

こてんぱん ⓒ beating; thrashing

🅰 ◎〜に遣っ付ける tear into sb; slam into sb; give it to sb. ◎〜に負ける be given a sound thrashing; be beaten to a pulp.

こてんこてん ⓒ beating; thrashing

🅰 ◎〜にやられた ◎ be beaten to a pulp; be given a sound thrashing.

ことこと clattering; rattling

🅰 〜(と)煮込む simmer sth for a long time. 箱の中で〜(と)音がした something rattled inside the box.

ゴトゴト　　　　　　　　　　　　　　　ゴリゴリ

ごとごと clopping; clattering
[Av] 列車が〜(と)通った the train clattered past. 〜(と)音を立てる鍋の湯 hot water prattling away in a pot. 天井で何かが〜(と)音がする something moves behind the ceiling.

ことん clonk; clink; thump
[Av] 〜と落ちる fall (over) with a thump. 〜と寝てしまう fall fast asleep. ②杖を〜と叩く thump (the floor with) one's walking stick.

ごにょごにょ mumbling; muttering
[Av] 〜(と)作戦を話す secretly discuss one's strategy. 〜(と)話す mumble; mutter.
[AJ] 〜(と)した話し方 a mumbling way of speaking. 〜(と)した事情 an unintelligible situation.
▸ ぶすぶす ▸ ぼそぼそ

こぽこぽ prattling; bubbling
[Av] コーヒーがパーコレーターで〜(と)沸く the coffee is prattling in the percolator.
▸ あぶあぶ

ごほごほ coughing; hacking
[Av] 〜(と)咳をする cough lightly; have a light cough.
▸ げほげほ ▸ ごほん ▸ こんこん

ごぼごぼ gurgling; bubbling
[Av] 〜と湧き出る温泉 a bubbling onsen.

ごほん(ごほん) cough; coff-coff
[Av] 〜と咳をする cough; let out a cough.
▸ げほげほ ▸ ごほごほ ▸ こんこん

こまごま [細々] minutely; in detail
[Av] 〜(と)述べる relate sth in great detail. 〜(と)立ち働く work fastidiously.
[AJ] 〜(と)した detailed; minute.
▸ ほそぼそ [細々]

ごみごみ messy; squalid
[AJ] 〜(と)した繁華街 a squalid shopping area. 〜(と)した部屋 a cluttered room; a messy room.
▸ ごしゃごしゃ

こりこり crisp; firm; stiff
[AJ] 〜した歯触り a crunchy bite.
[する] 〜する be crunchy. 首筋が〜する have a stiff neck.
▸ かりかり ▸ ぼりぼり

ごりごり scraping; crunching
[Av] 首を回すと〜(と)音がする I hear a crunching sound (in my neck) when I turn my head. 鼠が〜(と)壁をかじている the mice are gnawing

on the wall. 鍋を束子で〜(と)擦る scrub a pan with a scrubbing brush.
Ⓐ 〜しと兵児帯 a thick waistband.

ころころ rolling; roly-poly; chirping

Ⓐv 林檎が〜(と)転がった the apple rolled over. 話が〜(と)変わった the topics changed in rapid succession. 〜(と)太った赤ちゃん a chubby little baby. 〜(と)鳴る蟋蟀 a chirping cricket. 〜(と)笑う laugh merrily.

♦ からから ♦ げたげた ♦ けらけら

ごろごろ rumbling; purring

Ⓐv 岩が〜(と)転がり落ちた rocks fell down with a loud rumble. 遠ざかる雷が〜鳴りだした a peal of thunder rolled in the distance. 猫が喜んで〜(と)鳴った the cat purred with delight.
Ⓢ 〜する be idle; lie around; ⓒ loaf one's time away.

♦ がらがら ♦ ごーごー

ころっ easily; suddenly; utterly

Ⓐv ゴルフボールが〜と穴に入った the golf ball dropped into the hole. 〜と騙された be totally fooled; be completely taken in. 〜と忘れてしまう completely forget about *sth*; totally slip one's mind. 〜と負けた be utterly beaten; be beaten hands down. 〜と寝てしまう fall fast asleep.

ころり easily; suddenly; utterly

Ⓐv ベッドに〜(と)転がる drop into bed; roll into one's bed. 〜(と)いってしまう pass away suddenly; ⓒ drop dead. 〜(と)忘れてしまう completely forget about *sth*; totally slip one's mind. 〜(と)負ける be easily beaten; be beaten hands down. 彼は美人に〜(と)参った he fell head over heels for the beauty.

ごろり slumping; flopping

Ⓐv 〜(と)床に寝転ぶ collapse on the floor. 〜(と)横になる throw oneself down; flop down (on the floor).

♦ へこへこ

こわごわ trembling; fearful

Ⓐv 古井戸を〜と除く peer fearfully into the old well. 彼が〜と体を動かした he moved timidly.
Ⓐ 〜(と)した表情 a fearful expression. 〜した足取りで with timid steps. 〜(と)した様子 a state of terror; a fearful look.
Ⓢ 〜する be intimidated; be fearful; be afraid; be terrified.

♦ びくびく ♦ わなわな

ごわごわ stiff; starchy

Ⓐ 〜(と)したジーンズ stiff jeans; starched jeans. 〜(と)した手触り feel stiff.

ゴワゴワ / サクサク

Ⓝ 〜のタオル a starched towel.
♦ がびがび

こん knocking; rapping; yelping
Ⓐv テーブルを〜と打つ knock on the table. 狐が〜と鳴く the fox yelps.

ごん thud; thump; bump
Ⓐv 〜と壁にぶつける bump into a wall.
♦ がつん ♦ ごつん ♦ どかっ ♦ どっか

こんがり well-done; browned
Ⓐv 〜(と)焼けたフランスパン well toasted french bread.

こんこん knocking; tapping
Ⓐv ドアを〜とノックする knock the door. 〜と鳴く yelp. 〜と咳をする give a dry cough.
♦ げほげほ ♦ ごほごほ ♦ ごほん

こんこん [昏々] fast asleep
Ⓐv 〜と眠る be fast asleep.

こんこん [滾々] Ⓔ copious; gushing
Ⓐv Ⓔ 〜と流れる Ⓔ gush forth.
♦ どくどく

こんこん [懇々] repeatedly
Ⓐv 〜と諭してやる admonish sb; Ⓘ give sb a dressing-down. 〜と頼む request sth earnestly.

ごんごん banging; clanging
Ⓐv 拳でドアを〜とノックする bang the door with one's fist. 寺鐘〜と鳴った the temple bell sounded.
♦ からんからん ♦ こーん

こんもり thickly; densely
Ⓐv 〜(と)茂った山腹 a thickly-wooded hillside.
Ⓐj 〜(と)した森 a dense forest.

さ

ざーざー rushing; pouring
Ⓐv 〜水を掛ける shower sth with water. 雨が〜降る pour down with rain; Ⓒ Ⓘ rain cats and dogs. 音が〜(と)鳴る Ⓒ Ⓘ make a din of a noise.
♦ ざんざん ♦ どしゃどしゃ

ざーっ rushing; swooshing
Ⓐv 波が〜と砂浜に押し寄せてきた the waves rushed hit the beach with a swoosh. 滝の〜という音 the sound of a rushing waterfall.
♦ ざざっ

さくさく crisp; crunchy; skillfully
Ⓐv 〜(と)新雪を踏んだ the snow crunched underfoot.
Ⓐj 苹果がまだ〜している the apples are still crunchy.

ざくざく crunching; coarse; rough

[Av] キャベツを〜(と)切る cut through a cabbage. 野菜を〜に切る chop the vegetables up (into big chunks). 霜柱を〜(と)踏む crush the ice needles underfoot.

♦ ざっくざっく

さくっ lob; chop; rough; loosely

[Av] 大根を〜と切る chop the *daikon* in half. 〜と斜め読みする read sth cursory/diagonally. 〜と分かる have a rough understanding of sth.

♦ ざっ ♦ ざっくり ♦ ばっさり

ざざっ swooshing; swishing

[Av] 波が〜と防波堤に打ち寄せてきた the waves crashed against the breakwater.

♦ ざーっ

さっ quickly; suddenly

[Av] 窓を〜と開ける fling open a window. 打撃に〜と身をかわす quickly dodge a blow. 〜と目の前に現れる suddenly appear in front of one's eyes.

ざっ roughly; cursory; briefly

[Av] 〜と目を通す look over sth cursorily. 〜と掃除をする perfunctory cleaning. 問題に〜と触れる touch briefly on a matter. 〜と水をかける pour lots of water on sth; drench sth in water. 〜と説明する explain sth briefly.

[Aj] 〜とした話 a brief chat. 〜とした見積もり a rough estimate. 〜とした感想 a general impression.

[N] ⓒ 〜とこんなもんです this is what is boils down to.

♦ ざっくっ ♦ ざっくり

ざっくざっく crunching; crashing

[Av] 砂利の上を〜(と)行進すり march over the crunching gravel. キャベツを〜(と)切る tear through a cabbage. パチンコの玉が〜(と)出てきた the Pachinko pellets came pouring forth.

♦ ざくざく

ざっくばらん frank; candid; direct

[Av] 〜に事を言う speak frankly; ⓒ call a spade a spade.

[Aj] 〜とした人柄 (have) a frank disposition; be outspoken.

♦ ずけずけ ♦ ずばずば ♦ ずばり

ざっくり roughly; loosely; deeply

[Av] 〜と割れた傷口 a gaping wound. 包丁を〜と突っ込む thrust in a knife in deep. 〜と着こなす wear (a garment) casually.

[Aj] 〜とした解説 a loose explanation. 〜としたセーター a roughly

knit pull-over. 〜とした話し合い a general consultation.
N 〜とこんな感じです this is what it boils down to.

♦ ざくっ ♦ ざっ ♦ ゆるゆる

さっさ quickly; promptly

Av 〜と歩く walk quickly; keep up a brisk pace. 宿題を〜と片付ける get one's homework finished in no time.

♦ とっと

さっぱり entirely; neat; clean

Av 〜(と)忘れてしまう forget all about *sth*; let *sth* totally slip one's mind. © 〜分からない be unable to make sense of *sth*.
Aj 〜(と)した味 an uncomplicated taste. 〜(と)した食事 a light meal. 〜(と)した人柄 (have) an an easy-going personality; (have) a fine character. 〜(と)した部屋 a tidy room.
N 試験の成績は〜だ the exam results are dismal.
する 〜(と)する feel refreshed; feel relieved.

♦ あっさり ♦ すっきり

さばさば relieved; frank

Aj 〜(と)した態度 be frank, be openhearted.
する 〜する feel refreshed; be relieved; be unburdened.

ざぶざぶ slashing; sloshing

Av 顔を〜(と)洗う wash one's face with lots of water. 小川を〜と渡る slosh through the stream.

さめざめ sorrowful; anguished

Av 〜と泣く weep silently; weep bitterly; cry one's eyes out.

♦ しくしく ♦ めそめそ

さやさや rustling; whispering

Av 木の葉が〜(と)鳴っている the leaves rustle (in the wind). 篠竹が風で〜(と)触れ合っていた the bamboo grass rustled in the wind.

♦ さわさわ ♦ そよそよ

さらさら rustling; murmuring

Av 風で〜(と)音を立てる rustle in the wind. 〜(と)流れる小川 a murmuring brook. 〜(と)書く write nimbly; ⓘ write *sth* off the cuff. ⓔ have a facile pen.
Aj 〜(と)した髪 dry and easy falling hair. 〜(と)した雪 powdery snow.

♦ さわさわ ♦ そよそよ

ざらざら course; gritty; granular

Av ⓐ 〜(と)立ち行く do *sth* forthwith.
Aj 〜(と)した声 a gruff voice. 〜(と)した布 course cloth.
する 〜する be rough/course.

♦ ざりざり ♦ じゃらじゃら

さらっ smoothly; forthrightly

[Av] 刀を〜と受け流す parry sb's sword smoothly. 失敗を〜と忘れる put one's failure easily behind one.
[Aj] 〜とした切れ地 smooth cloth; cloth with a silky texture. ⓒ 〜とした人柄 an an easy-going personality.

さらり smoothly; thinly; entirely

[Av] 〜と水に流す let *sth* go easily. 批判を〜とかわす parry sb's criticism with ease. タバコを〜とやめる give up smoking just like that.
[Aj] 〜とした空気 crisp air. 〜とした油 smooth oil. 〜とした性格 (have) an an easy-going personality.

♦ すいすい ♦ すらすら ♦ するする

ざりざり gritty; course; rough

[Av] 〜(と)砂を踏む walk in the course sand.
[Aj] 〜(と)した布 course cloth.
[する] 〜する be rough/course.

♦ ざらざら ♦ じゃらじゃら

さわさわ [爽々] rustling; clearly

[Av] 秋風が〜(と)木を吹き抜けた the autumn breeze rustled through the trees. 〜(と)いう音 a rustling sound. ⓐ 胸が〜(と)落ち着かない be ill at ease (about *sth*).
[N] ⓐ 心地〜となる feel refreshed.

♦ さやさや ♦ さらさら ♦ そよそよ

ざわざわ rustle; bustle; noise

[Av] 森が〜(と)音を立てる the woods are alive with the rustle (of leaves and branches).
[Aj] 〜(と)している会場 a bustling meeting place.
[する] 〜する ❶ rustle; bustle. ❷ have goose pimples; have goosebumps.

♦ がやがや ♦ わいわい ♦ わーわー

さんさん [燦々] brilliantly; brightly

[Av] 〜と太陽の光を浴びる bask in the sunshine; be bathed in sunlight.

♦ こうこう [煌々] ♦ さんらん [燦爛]

さんさん [潸々] [A] pouring steadily

[Av] ⓐ 〜と流れる涙 a steady flow of tears. ⓐ 雨が〜と落ちた it rained incessantly.

ざんざん pouring heavily

[Av] 雨が〜と降った the rain came down thick and fast.

♦ ざーざー ♦ どしゃどしゃ

ざんぶり splash; plop

[Av] 波が〜(と)返す音 the sound of breaking waves. 〜(と)海に飛び込む dive into the sea.

♦ じゃぶり ♦ どぶん

さんらん [燦爛] 国 brilliantly

- A ⓔ ～として輝く shine brightly; shine brilliantly.
- N ⓔ ～たる brilliant; lustrous; radiant.

♦ こうこう [煌々] ♦ さんさん [燦々]

し

しーっ shhh!; shoo!

- A 鴉を～と追い払った I shooed off the crows.

じーじー shrill; whining; sizzling

- A 蝉が～(と)鳴く the cicada is shrilling. 鉄板焼きの肉が～(と)焼ける the *teppanyaki* meat is sizzling.

♦ じゅーじゅー

じーっ intently; patiently

- A 猫が～と鳥を見つめた the cat followed the bird's every move.

しーん silently; quietly

- A ～と静まり返る fall utterly silent.
- A ～とした闇の中 the stillness of the night.
- する ～とする be utterly still; be dead silent.

じーん numbing; heartrending

- A ～と(胸に)来る be heartrending;

be touched to the core. 指が～と痺れた my fingers were numb with the cold. 目頭が～と熱くなった I felt tears well up in my eyes.

しおしお [悄々] dejected; sad

- A ～(と)家に帰る return home with a heavy heart. ～(と)退場する make a sad exit.

♦ すごすご

ジグリグ zig-zag; meandering

- A ～(と)した細道 a winding path.
- N UFOが～の動きで飛んで行った the UFO flew off in a zig-zag movement. 山に入ると道が～になった once among the mountains, the road began to meander.
- A ～(と)している波形 a zig-zag (triangle) waveform.

♦ うねうね ♦ ジグサグ

しくしく sobbing; pain; incessant

- A ～(と)泣く sob/weep. ～(と)痛む have a persistent/griping pain.
- する 腹が～する have a groping stomach ache.

♦ さめざめ ♦ めそめそ

じくじく oozing; welling; sodden

- A 傷口から～(と)膿が出る puss oozes from the wound.
- A 年中～(と)している土地 land that

oozes water throughout the year.
する ～する傷口 an oozing wound.

しげしげ [繁々] frequently; often
Av ～(と)居酒屋へ足を運ぶ frequent an *izakaya*. 彼は～(と)その店に通う he frequently visits that shop. ～(と)彼女の顔を見た he looked hard at her; he fixed his eyes on her.

▶ たびたび [度々] ▶ ひんぴん [頻々]

しこしこ chewy; springy; steadily
Av ～(と)作曲を書き続ける make steady progress on one's (musical) composition; work away at one's composition. © ～(と)勉強する plug away at one's studies.
Aj ～(と)した歯触り be chewy; (have) a chewy consistency.
する Ⓥ ⓢ ～する masturbate; Ⓥ ⓢ jerk off.

▶ もちもち

しずしず [静々] quietly; slowly
Av 葬列は～(と)進んだ the funeral procession moved along quietly.

▶ そろそろ ▶ ぼつぼつ

じたばた struggle; wriggle; wrestle
する ～する struggle; wrestle. 今さら～しても始まらない it's too late to make a scene now. ～すると殺すぞ move and you're dead!

じっ motionlessly; fixedly; firmly
Av 鳥を～と見つめた gaze at a bird. 先生を～と聞いている listen intently to the teacher. ～と考え込む be lost in thought.
Aj ～としている be still; sit still.

しっかり tightly; firmly; fully
Av 縄を～(と)縛る fasten a rope tight. ～(と)勉強する study hard. ～(と)覚えておく remember *sth* well.
Aj ～(と)した研究 thorough research. ～(と)した造り a solid build. ～(と)した青年 a steady young man.
する ～する do *sth* thoroughly.

▶ がっちり ▶ きっちり

しっくり exactly; nicely
Av 彼女と姑との間が～(と)行った she and her mother-in-law got along well. 原文の意味に～(と)合う convey the exact meaning of the original text.
する ～する be fitting; be more like it; go well with *sth*.

じっくり deliberately; carefully
Av ～(と)腰をすえる settle down (to do *sth*); © buckle down (to do *sth*). 案を～(と)考える think the plan over carefully.

しずしず [静々] ᴇ quetly; slowly
- Ⓐ ⓒ 〜(と)進む proceed gracefully.

しっとり calm; gently; damp
- Ⓐ 汗で〜(と)濡れている be wet with perspiration.
- Ⓐⱼ 〜とした damp; wet; moist. 〜とした気分で in a quiet mood. 〜とした感じの女性 a graceful woman.
- 🈚 〜する be damp/moist.
- ♦ しとしと ♦ じめじめ

じっとり wet; soaked; drenched
- Ⓐ 汗で〜(と)汗ばんだ be drenched with perspiration.
- Ⓐⱼ 〜とした drenched; soaked. ⓐ 〜とした気分で in a quiet mood. ⓐ 〜とした感じの女性 a graceful woman.
- 🈚 〜する be drenched/sodden.

しっぽり drenched; fondly; slowly
- Ⓐ 恋人と一夜を〜(と)語り明かす talk the night away with one's love. 〜(と)濡れる ❶ be drenched. ⓒ ❷ be in (deeply) in love; ⓘ be head over heels.
- Ⓐⱼ 〜とした be drenched; be soaked.
- 🈚 〜する ❶ be drenched/sodden. ❷ unwind; feel at ease; spend quality time (with sb/sth).

しとしと gently; moist; damp
- Ⓐ 春雨が〜(と)降っている a gentle spring rain is falling. ⓐ 母が〜(と)階段を上がってきた mother came up the stairs quietly. 霞に〜(と)濡れている be drenched by the mist.
- Ⓐⱼ 〜とした雨 gentle rain. 〜とした朝 a wet morning.
- 🈚 〜する be damp/moist.
- ♦ しずしず ♦ しっとり ♦ じめじめ

じとじと drenched; soaked
- Ⓐ 汗で〜(と)汗ばんだ be drenched with perspiration.
- Ⓐⱼ 〜とした下着 drenched underwear.
- 🈚 〜する be drenched/sodden
- ♦ じっとり ♦ しっぽり

しなしな soft; flexible; pliant
- Ⓐ 草が〜(と)折れた be grass folded softly. 枝が〜(と)撓む be branch bent pliantly. 〜(と)歩く walk with a spring. 茎が〜(と)萎れた the stems grew soft and withered.
- Ⓐⱼ ⓐ 〜(と)した女 a pliant woman.
- ♦ なよなよ

しばしば blinking; often
- Ⓐ 〜起こる occur frequently. 〜現れる show up regularly.
- 🈚 目を〜させる blink with one's eyes.
- ♦ たびたび ♦ ちょくちょく

しみじみ [沁々] keenly; deeply

- 友達と〜(と)語り合う have a heartfelt talk with one's friend(s). 〜(と)感じる feel sth keenly. 〜(と)反省する feel deep remorse.

♦ じんみり ♦ つくづく

じめじめ clammy; gloomy

- 〜(と)した空気 humid air. 〜(と)した土地 moist soil. 薄暗く〜(と)した日々 dank and gloomy days. 〜(と)した梅雨 the damp and humid rain season. 〜(と)した話 a sad story. 汗で〜(と)した下着 underwear clammy with sweat. 〜(と)した会話 a depressing conversation.

♦ しずしず ♦ しっとり ♦ しとしと

しゃーしゃー swoosh; brazenly

- 〜している be unperturbed; stay cool; act as if nothing had happened. 〜(と)いう水音が聞こえる hear the rush of water. 〜と嘘をつく tell lies without batting an eye.

♦ しゅーしゅー

じゃーじゃー gushing; splashing

- 〜(と)水を掛ける splash sth with water. 水が〜(と)出てきた the water gushed forth. 雨が〜(と)降ってきた the rain started to come down in torrents.

♦ ちゃぽちゃぽ ♦ ぽちゃぽちゃ

じゃぶん plunging; splashing

- 〜とプールに飛び込む enter the pool with a splash.

♦ ざんぶり ♦ どぶん

じゃぼん plunging; splashing

- そのまま〜と浸かってしまう be submerged in one big gulp.

♦ ざんぶり ♦ どぶん

じゃかじゃか banging; blaring

- ギターを〜鳴らす slam away on a guitar. お金を〜使う spend (one's) money freely; have a hole in one's hand.

しゃきしゃき crisp; precisely

- 〜(と)事を運ぶ do sth precisely; do sth efficiently. 〜(と)返事をする give a crisp answer.
- 〜(と)したレタス crisp lettuce. 〜(と)した歯ざわり a crunchy bite. 〜(と)した職人 a skilled artisan.

しゃくしゃく [綽々] ample; easy

- 〜たる余裕 easy and grace.

しゃっきり crisp; straight; briskly

- 〜(と)背筋を伸ばす stand up straight.
- 〜(と)した食感 a crunchy bite. 〜(と)した老人 a brisk old (wo)man.
- 〜しなさい stand up straight!

しゃなりしゃなり gracefully

[Av] ⓐ 〜(と)歩く walk gracefully.

じゃぶじゃぶ splashing; swishing

[Av] 〜(と)浅瀬を渡る splash through a shallows. 足を〜(と)お風呂洗う splash one's feet around in a bath. お金を〜使う spend (one's) money freely; have a hole in one's hand. 株で〜(と)お金を儲ける rake it in at the stock exchange.

♦ ちゃぽちゃぽ ♦ ぽちゃぽちゃ

じゃらじゃら jingling; dally; flirt

[する] 小銭を〜させる make the coins jingle. ⓓ 人前で〜するな don't act so lewd in public! ⓓ 〜物言うな stop jibbering; don't talk nonsense!

[する] 〜する dally; flirt. 〜するカップル a flirtatious couple. 彼氏と〜する ⓒ make out with one's boyfriend.

♦ ちゃりん ♦ ちりんちりん

じゃりじゃり gritty; course; rough

[Av] 〜(と)砂を踏む walk in the gritty pebbles.

[Aj] 〜(と)した布 course cloth.

[する] 〜する be rough; be gritty.

♦ ざらざら ♦ ざりざり

しゃん in shape; dignified; orderly

[Av] 体を〜と起こす stand up straight; straighten one's back.

[Aj] 〜としている be in good shape; carry oneself well. 〜とした家 an orderly household. 〜とした姿勢 a dignified posture. 〜とした生活を送る lead an orderly life.

[する] 〜としなさい pull yourself together; get a hold on yourself.

♦ ちゃん

しゃんしゃん jingling; robust

[Av] 〜(と)鈴を鳴らす jingle a bell. 〜(と)片付ける get things in order.

[Aj] 〜としている be in good shape; be quite sprightly.

じゃんじゃん clanging; non-stop

[Av] 早鐘が〜(と)打ち鳴らす ring the morning bell continuously. 〜金を使う spend money like water. 電話が〜(と)鳴る the telephone rings incessantly.

♦ どしどし ♦ どんどん

しゅーしゅー rustling; hissing

[Av] ⓒ 衣服の〜(と)鳴る音 the rustling of clothes. ガスが〜(と)漏れていた the gas escaped with a hiss.

♦ しゃーしゃー

じゅーじゅー sizzling; frizzling

[Av] 肉が〜(と)焼けている the meat is sizzling (in the frying pan).

♦ じーじー

しゅくしゅく [粛々] ᴇ silently
- N ⓒ ～たる silently; hushed.
- ◆ちんちん [沈々]

じゅっ sizzling; frizzling
- Av 鍛冶屋が熱した刀を～と水に入れた the swordsmith plunged the red-hot sword into the water.

しゅっしゅっ chug-chug; brushing
- Av 汽車が～（と）走った the steam engine chugged along. ～（と）靴を磨く brush up one's shoes.

しゅるしゅる rustling; slithering
- Av エレベーターが～（と）音を立てて降りてきた the elevator came down with a whiz. 新幹線が～（と）ホームに滑り込んできた the *shinkansen* came gliding in along the platform.
- ◆にゅるにゅる

しゅんしゅん hissing; whistling
- Av 湯が～（と）沸いていた the water was boiling.

しょぼしょぼ drizzling; gloomily
- Av その夜雨が～（と）降った that night it drizzled.
- Aj ～（と）した目 bleary-eyed. ～（と）した姿 a disheveled look.
- する 目が～する blink weakly.
- ◆そぼそぼ

じょりじょり scrape; shave
- Av ～（と）襟足を剃る shave the hairline along the neck. 顎髭を～（と）触る scratch one's beard.
- Aj ～（と）した感覚 a scratching sensation.
- ◆そりぞり

しょんぼり dejectedly; gloomily
- Av ～（と）帰る return crestfallen.
- Aj ～（と）した姿 a crestfallen look.
- する ～する feel depressed; ⓒ ① be down in the dumps.

じりじり ringing; slowly; sizzling
- Av 目覚ましの音が～（と）鳴った the alarm went off. ～（と）敵に迫る close in on the enemy. 劣勢を～（と）盛り返す steadily rally from an inferior position. 株が～（と）値上がりした the stocks gradually rose. □□□□□□ □□□ ～（と）照りつける太陽 the scorching sun.
- する ～する grow impatient. ～しながら待つ wait impatiently.
- ◆いらいら ◆むしゃくしゃ

じろじろ staring; scrutinizing
- Av ～（と）人の顔を見る stare at *sb's* face. 上から下まで～（と）見る scrutinize *sb* from top to toe.
- ◆まじまじ ◆じろり ◆まんじり

じろっ staring; scrutinizing
- Av ～と男の顔を見る stare/glare at the man's face.

じろり staring; glancing
- Av ～と顔を見る stare at *sb's* face; cast a sharp glance at *sb's* face. ～と一瞥する stare at *sb/sth*; cast a sharp glance at *sb/sth*.
- ♦ じろじろ ♦ まじまじ ♦ まんじり

じわじわ slowly; oozing; seeping
- Av 借金が～(と)増えた the debts grew steadily. 汚染が～(と)広がった the pollution gradually spread.

しん silence; stillness; piercing
- Av ～と静まる fall silent; become still. 寒さが～と体に染み込んだ the cold pierced my bones.
- Aj ～とした森 the silent forest. ～とした寒さ biting cold. ～とした音 a piercing sound.
- N ～となる become silent; fall silent.
- ♦ ぞくぞく ♦ ひんやり

じん numbing; heartrending
- Av 手足が～と痺れた my limbs were numb (with cold). ～と痺れる指先 (have) numb fingers. 胸に～とくる光景 a heartrending scene. 彼女の言葉が～と胸にきた her words pierced my heart.

しんしん [深々] 国 deeply
- N ⓒ ～たる問題 a profound problem.

じんじん tingling; throbbing
- Av 足が～(と)痺れる my legs feel numb. こめかみが～(と)痛む my temples throb with pain. 耳が～(と)なり始めた my ears began to ring.
- する 腫れた傷口が～する the swollen wound throbs with pain.
- ♦ がんがん ♦ ずきずき ♦ ずきん

しんなり soft; supple; pliant
- Aj ～(と)した動作 lithe movements. ～(と)した皮 supple leather.
- する ～させる soften *sth* up.

しんねり slowly; persistently
- Aj ⓐ ～(と)した口調で話す talk slowly and deliberately.

しんねりむっつり morose; sullen
- Aj ⓐ ～(と)した男 a morose man.
- ♦ ぶすり ♦ むっつり

じんみり seriously; solemnly
- Av ⓒ ～(と)語り合う have a serious talk.
- Aj ⓒ 皆が～(と)した everyone was lost in thought.
- ♦ しみじみ ♦ つくづく

じんわり slowly; gradually

[A] 涙が～と彼女の目に浮かんだ tears slowly welled up in her eyes. ～と胸に伝わってきた slowly it sank in. ～と目の奥が熱くなった I felt my eyes sting with tears.

す

すいすい smoothly; unhindered

[A] ～(と)氷の上を滑っていく glide along over the ice. 問題が～(と)解決した the problem was smoothly ironed out. 仕事を～(と)片付けた the work was competed without a hitch.

♦ さらり ♦ すらすら ♦ するする

すーすー hissing; slurping

[A] ⓢ ～(と)ラーメンを食べる slurp one's noodles.

♦ ずるずる

すーっ slurp; suck; straight; gently

[A] 空気が～と抜けた the air escaped with a hiss. 汗が～と背中から流れた sweat poured down his back in a straight line. ～と伸びた枝 a perfectly straight branch. 列車が～と止まった the train came to a smooth stop. 毛先まで～と纏まる smoothen out one's hair into the tips.

[A] 胸が～とした regain one's composure; calm down.

すかすか wide; cleanly; smoothly

[A] ⓒ ～と切る cut sth clean off.
[N] このズボンは～だ these trousers are baggy. 箱は～だ the box is too large. 蜜柑は～だ the tangerine is dry. 髪は～だ my hair feels smooth. 老人の骨が～になる the bones of the elderly become brittle.

すかっ refreshed; clear; clean

[A] 胸が～とした feel refreshed. ～とした切れ味 (have) a good cut. ⓒ ～とした身なり be stylishly dressed.
[する] ～とする be refreshing.

♦ すっ ♦ すぱっ ♦ ずぶっ

ずきずき smarting; throbbing

[A] 傷が～(と)痛む the wound smarts terribly.
[する] 頭が～する have a bad headache; ⓒ have a splitting headache.

♦ がんがん ♦ じんじん

ずきん throbbing; smarting

[A] 後悔で～胸がと痛む feel a pang of remorse. 頭が～痛む have a throbbing headache.
[する] 頭が～する have a bad headache; ⓒ have a splitting headache.

♦ がんがん ♦ ずきずき ♦ じんじん

すくすく quickly; rapidly; fast

[Av] ～(と)伸びる grow tall quickly; grow with the day. ～(と)育つ grow up rapidly. ～(と)大きくなる grow tall quickly; grow up fast.

ずけずけ bluntly; frankly

[Av] 思った事を～(と)言う bluntly speak what is on one's mind. ～(と)悪口を言う speak ill of sb without shame. ～(と)物を言う say whatever is on one's mind.
[Aj] ～した言い方 a blunt way of speaking.

♦ ざっくばらん ♦ ずばずば ♦ ずばり

すごすご dejected; down; sad

[Av] ～(と)帰ってくる come away disheartened. ～(と)退場する exit a contest in low spirits. ～(と)引き下げる leave dejectedly.

♦ しおしお

ずしっ heavily; profoundly

[Av] ～と家計に響く weigh heavily on the family budget. 肩に～と来る weigh heavily on one's shoulders.

♦ ずっしり ♦ どっしり

ずずん rumble; vibration; heavy

[Av] 船が～と傾く list heavily. 地震の音が～と響いた the earthquake made a deep rumble. 戦車が～と道を通った the tanks thundered through the streets. ◎ ～と落ち込む grow despondent; sink into a (deep) depression.

すたこら scurry; helter-skelter

[Av] ～(と)逃げ出す scurry away.

すたすた briskly; quickly

[Av] ～(と)歩く walk briskly; keep up a brisk pace. ～(と)歩き出す set off at a brisk pace.

♦ きびきび ♦ てきぱき ♦ ぱきぱき

ずたずた [寸々] torn; cut up

[Av] 手紙を～に裂く tear a letter to pieces. 服が～に裂けた the dress was all torn up.
[Aj] 身も心も～だ be broken, both in spirit and in body.
[N] ～になる be cut up; be shredded; be torn up; be ripped to pieces.

♦ つだつだ [寸々]

すっ straight; swiftly; refreshed

[Av] ～と伸びる枝 a branch growing straight. ～と消える disappear suddenly; disappear without a trace. 息を～と吸い込む draw in a deep breath of air.
[する] 胸が～とする be refreshing; feel good.

♦ すかっ ♦ すぱっ ♦ ずぶっ

スッカリ / スッポリ

すっかり completely; totally
- Av ～忘れる forget *sth* completely. 気分が～良くなった feel much better; feel quite recovered. 家が～出来上がった the house was completely finished. ～ご無沙汰している haven't been in touch for a long time. もう～嫌になる be sick and tired of *sb/sth*.

すっきり refreshed; plainly, neatly
- Av 和服を～(と)着こなす wear (one's) Japanese dress with ease/skill/style.
- Aj ～(と)した味 a refreshing taste. ～(と)した文章 lucid writing. ～(と)したデザイン a refined design. 服装が～している be dressed neatly; be trimly dressed.
- する ～する feel refreshed; feel clear-headed. ～しない話 a muddled story.
- ♦ あっさり ♦ さっぱり

ずっしり heavily; dignified
- Av ～(と)構える assume a dignified air. その言葉が～(と)胸に応えた those words hit home hard. ～(と)地響きがした there was a deep underground rumble.
- Aj ～(と)した重いカバン a heavy handbag. ～(と)した人物 a person of great composure; an unflappable person. ～(と)した構え a dignified air. ～(と)した風貌 a dignified appearance.
- ♦ ずしっ ♦ どっしり

すってんころり fall down flat
- Av Ⓐ ～(と)転ぶ fall down flat. Ⓐ ～(と)尻餅をつく land on one's rear end.
- ♦ すてん

すってんてん penniless; flat broke
- N ～になる lose all one's money; blow all one's money; Ⓒ become flat broke. ～だ be penniless; Ⓒ be flat broke; Ⓒ be stone-broke.

すっぱり totally; wholly; cleanly
- Av 彼は梅の枝を～(と)切り落とした he lobbed off the whole branch. 彼女は～(と)タバコをやめた she quit smoking altogether.
- ♦ きっぱり ♦ はっきり ♦ ばっさり

すっぽり entirely; completely
- Av 町が一面～(と)雪を に覆われた the whole town was covered in (a thick blanket of) snow. 人形の首が～(と)取れてしまった the doll's head was torn right off. カメラが～(と)カバンに嵌った the camera fitted right into the carrying bag.
- ♦ すぽっ

すてん fall down flat

Av ～と転ぶ fall down flat (on one's face). 波に～と足を攫われる be swept of one's feet by a wave.

♦ すってんころり

すとん plunk; plonk; come down

Av ～と落ちる fall down with a thud. 温度が～と下がった the fever came right down; the temperature suddenly dropped/plummeted.

ずどん thud; bang; boom

Av ～と一発撃つ fire a (single) shot. 塀に～とぶつかる slam into a wall.

すぱすぱ puff-puff; lightly

Av タバコを～と吸う puff away at one's cigarette. 大根を～と切る chop up a *daikon*. 問題を～と片付ける solve a problem just like that.

♦ ぶかぶか

ずばずば bluntly; outspoken

Av ものを～と言う speak bluntly; be outspoken; be frank; ⓘ call a spade a spade. ～と(と)指示を出す give instructions without hesitating.

♦ ざっくばらん ♦ ずけずけ ♦ ずばり

すぱっ entirely; thoroughly

Av ⓒ 会社を～と辞める quit one's job just like that. 青竹を～と割る split young bamboo right down the middle. ～と言い切る state one's case resolutely; say *sth* out of the blue.

♦ すかっ ♦ すっ ♦ ずぶっ

ずばり decisively; precisely

Av ⓒ 木を～(と)切り倒す fell a tree with one bold stroke. 問題を～(と)言い当てる get straight to the crux of a problem; ⓘ hit the nail on the head. ものを～(と)言う speak bluntly; be outspoken; call a spade a spade. ～(と)ⓘ痛い所を衝く boldly point out an issue's weak spot; touch on *sb*'s weak spot.

♦ ざっくばらん ♦ ずけずけ ♦ ずばずば

ずぶずぶ deeply; soaked; pissed

Av 足が泥の中に～(と)めり込む get stuck in the mud. ⓐ ～(と)酔っ払う become blind drunk; drink oneself into a stupor; ⓥ ⓢ get pissed. 針を～(と)刺す pierce *sth* with a needle.

ずぶっ totally; completely; wholly

Av 体を～とお風呂に沈み込ませる immerse one's whole body in a bath. ～と泥に吸い込まれる get bogged down in the mud.

♦ すかっ ♦ すっ ♦ ずぶっ

すべすべ [滑々] smooth; sleek

Aj ～(と)した髪 sleek/smooth hair.

スベスベ　　　　　　　　　　　　　　　　　　　　　　　ズラリ

〜（と）した床 a polished floor.
♦ つるつる ♦ のっぺり

すぽっ snugly; tightly; pop; plop
[Av] 栓が〜と抜けた the cork came out with a plop. 〜と箱に納まる fit snugly into the box.
♦ すっぽり

すやすや peacefully; soothing
[Av] ⓐ 〜（と）流れる風 a soothing wind. 赤ん坊が〜（と）眠っている the baby is sleeping peacefully.
[Aj] ⓐ 〜（と）した夜風 a soothing evening breeze.
♦ ぐーぐー ♦ ぐっすり

すらすら smoothly; easily; readily
[Av] ドイツ語を〜（と）話せる speak German with ease. 仕事が〜（と）運ぶ the work goes smoothly. 問題を〜（と）解決する solve a problem with ease. 〜（と）答える answer without (a moment's) hesitation.
♦ さらり ♦ すいすい ♦ するする

ずらずら successively; continuing
[Av] 結果が〜（と）表示された the results were displayed in rapid succession. 自転車が〜（と）並んだ the bicycles were lined up in a row. 条件を〜（と）並べ立てる list up one's conditions one after the

other. ⓒ 〜（と）文句を捏ねる quibble over an endless list of complaints. 日記に〜（と）その日の出来事を書く jot down one's daily experiences (one after the other) in one's diary.

すらっ long; slender; slim
[Aj] 〜とした美人 a slender beauty.

ずらっ in a line; in a row
[Av] 〜と並ぶ高級車 lined-up luxury cars. 〜と並んだLDK an apartment with the living room, dining room, and kitchen spaced close together.
♦ ずらり ♦ ぞろり ♦ ほっそり

すらり long; slender; smooth
[Av] 〜と刀を抜く draw one's sword in a flash. 障子を〜と開ける smoothly slide open the *shōji*. 話が〜と纏まった (they) easily came to an agreement.
[Aj] 〜とした青年 a slender youth.
♦ すらっ ♦ すんなり ♦ ほっそり

ずらり in a row; lined up
[Av] タクシーがホテルの前で〜と並んでいた cabs were lined up in front of the hotel. お歴々が〜と居並んだ the distinguished guests were (sitting) in a row.
♦ ずらっ ♦ ぞろり

するする smoothly; swiftly; nimbly

[Av] 幕が〜(と)上がった the curtains smoothly rose. 猿が〜(と)木に登った the monkey nimbly climbed the tree. 船が〜(と)岸を離れた the vessel swiftly left the shore behind. 結び目が〜(と)解けた the knot quickly came undone. このクリームは〜(と)肌に馴染む this cream is quickly and smoothly absorbed in the skin.

♦ さらり ♦ すいすい ♦ すらすら

ずるずる trailing; sliding; slurping

[Av] スープを〜(と)飲む slurp one's soup. 洟を〜(と)啜りあげる sniff up one's nasal mucus. 〜(と)決着を延ばす put off a decision. 〜(と)引き出す draw *sth* out slowly; let *sth* drag on. 泥濘んだ斜面を〜(と)滑り降りる slither down the muddy slope.

♦ すーすー ♦ つるつる

するり smoothly; unhindered

[Av] 彼女がドレスを〜と脱いだ she slipped off her dress. 彼が〜と部屋を抜け出した he slipped out of the room. 手から〜と逃げる slip through one's fingers.

すれすれ grazing; skimming; just

[Av] 〜に到着する arrive just on time. 水面〜に飛ぶ skim over the water. [N] 〜のところで間に合う be just in time. 弾丸は〜のところを飛んだ the bullet whistled past my ear.

♦ かすかす ♦ かつかつ

ずんぐり stout; stocky; rotund

[Aj] 〜(と)した子供 a dumpy child. 〜(と)した指 sausage-like fingers.

ずんずん rapidly; quickly; steadily

[Av] 〜(と)歩く keep up a brisk pace. ⊙ 仕事が〜(と)捗る make good progress (with one's work). 〜(と)大きくなる grow rapidly. 山が爆発で〜(と)響いた the mountains resounded with the sound of the explosion.

[Aj] 〜(と)した痛み ⊙ a nagging pain.

♦ ぐんぐん

すんなり slender; supple; smooth

[Av] 試験に〜(と)通る pass the exams without a glitch. 〜(と)妥結する reach an agreement without trouble. 議案が〜(と)通った the bill was passed unanimously. 条件を〜(と)受け入れる readily accept the conditions. 話が〜(と)纏まる come to an amicable agreement.

[Aj] ⊙ 〜(と)した手足 slender limbs. ⊙ 〜(と)した笹の葉 slender bamboo grass leaves.

♦ すらっ ♦ すらり ♦ ほっそり

せ

せいせい [清々] refreshed

する ～する feel refreshed; feel relieved.

ぜいぜい gasping; puffing; panting

A ～(と)喘ぐ gasp for air. 喉が喘息で～(と)鳴る wheeze with asthma.

♦ えんえん ♦ はーはー ♦ ふーふー

せかせか fidgety; agitatedly

A ～(と)歩き回る walk around nervously.
A ～(と)した話し方 an agitated manner of speaking.
する 気ばかりが～する get all worked up over sth.

せっせ diligently; industriously

A ～と働く work diligently.

♦ こつこつ

せんせん [潺々] E A murmuringly

A ⒸⒶ ～と流れる細川 a murmuring brook.

♦ そうそう [淙々]

そ

そうそう [錚々] E eminent

N ⒸⒶ ～たる学者 an eminent academic; a prominent scholar; a distinguished scholar.

そうそう [淙々] E A murmuringly

N ⒺⒶ ～たる小川 a murmuring stream; a babbling brooklet.

♦ せんせん [潺々]

ぞくぞく shivering; shuddering

する 風邪で～(と)する shiver with a cold. 寒さで～(と)する shiver with the cold. 背筋が～(と)する have shivers run down one's spine.

♦ しん ♦ ひんやり

ぞくぞく [続々] successively

A ～(と)来る pour in. ～(と)出る pour out. ～(と)出て来る appear one after the other; appear in rapid succession.

そっ softly; quietly; stealthily

A 障子を～と閉める gently close the shōji. ～と事を運ぶ do sth in secret; ① do sth on the sly. 皿を～と机に置く put the plates softly on the table. ～と歩く walk quietly.
する 問題を～としておく let a problem/matter rest.

ぞっ shuddering; shivering

する ～とする shudder/shiver. 考えただけで～とする shudder at the mere

idea. 〜とするほどの美人 a stunning beauty. 〜とするような話 a blood-curdling story.

ぞっこん entirely; completely

[する] ⓢ 〜に惚れ込む be deeply in love with sb; ⓘ have a crush on sb; ⓔ be infatuated with sb.
[N] ⓢ 彼は彼女に〜だ he is deeply in love with her; ⓘ he has a crush on her; ⓔ he is infatuated with her.

そぼそぼ drizzling

[Av] ⓐ 雨が〜(と)降っている it is drizzling.
♦ しょぼしょぼ

そよそよ gently; softly; breeze

[Av] 〜(と)吹く夏風 the gentle summer breeze. 木の葉が〜(と)揺れた the leaves rustled in the breeze.
♦ さらさら ♦ さらさら ♦ さわさわ

ぞりぞり scratch; scrape; shave

[Av] 〜(と)髭を剃る shave off one's mustache. 〜(と)痛みを感じる feel a smarting pain. ⓒ 毛虫が〜(と)動いた the caterpillar moved with a scratching sound.
♦ じょりじょり

そろそろ slowly; gradually; soon

[Av] 〜(と)歩く walk slowly/gingerly.

〜行こうか let's go; shall we be going? もう〜出発の時間だ it's already time to leave. 〜暗くなる it's already turning dark.
♦ しずしず ♦ ぼつぼつ

ぞろぞろ swarming; trailing

[Av] 蟻が〜(と)這う be swarming with ants. 人が〜(と)カフェに入ってきた people filed into the cafe. ⓐ ウエディングドレスの裾を〜(と)引き摺る drag the hem of the wedding dress across the floor.
♦ うざうざ ♦ うじゃうじゃ ♦ うようよ

ぞろり in a line; in a lump; sloppily

[Av] 学生たちが〜とバスから降りた the students filed out of the bus. 名士が〜と居並んだ the dignitaries were (sitting) in a row. ⓐ 彼はレインコートを〜と着ていた he wore the rain coat in a sloppy way.
♦ ずらっ ♦ ずらり

そわそわ restless; lively; fidgety

[Av] ⓒ 〜(と)落ち着かない be fidgety; be nervous; ⓘ be on tenterhooks; ⓒ ⓘ be on needles and pins.
[A] 〜(と)した人 a restless person. 発表待ちで立ったり座ったり〜している be unable to sit still in anticipation of the results.
♦ わさわさ

た

だーん bang; pang; crash
- ～と銃の音がした there was the bang of a gun. タワーが～と倒れた the tower toppled with a huge crash. 酔っ払いは～と障子に飛んで行った the drunkard crashed through the *shōji*.
- ♦ がたん ♦ どかん ♦ どん

だくだく gushing; thumping
- 汗が～(と)流れる ⓔ perspire profusely; ⓒ ⓘ sweat like a horse.

たじたじ recoiling; reeling
- 圧倒的な勢いに～となる buckle under the unrelenting pressure. 彼女の涙に～となった he was swayed by the woman's tears. ⓒ 選手の～となる腕前 the athlete's intimidating skill.
- ♦ もじもじ

たっぷり plenty; ample; full
- グラスに～(と)ワインを注ぐ fill a glass to the brim with wine. ～(と)食べてください please eat as much as you can. 時間は～(と)ある have plenty of time. ⓒ ～(と)二時間かかる it will take at least two hours.
- ～(と)した服 wide-fitting clothes; comfortable clothes.
- ～だ be in great supply; be full of *sth*; be sufficient.
- ♦ たんまり ♦ どっさり ♦ なみなみ

たびたび [度々] often; frequently
- ～外出する go out frequently. ～お邪魔する bother *sb* regularly.
- ♦ しげしげ [繁々] ♦ ひんぴん [頻々]

だぶだぶ loose; flabby; saggy
- ソースを～(と)かける cover *sth* with sauce; smother *sth* in sauce.
- ～(と)したズボン baggy trousers.
- ビールで腹が～(と)する feel the beer slosh around in one's stomach.
- ～の上着 a loose overcoat.
- ♦ ぶかぶか ♦ ぶよぶよ

たらたら dripping; slowly; gently
- ⓒ ～(と)お世辞を言う shower *sb* with compliments; ⓔ be obsequious in one's compliments. ～(と)汗を流す ⓔ perspire profusely; ⓒ ⓘ sweat like a horse.
- ♦ ぽたぽた ♦ ぽとぽと ♦ ぽろぽろ

だらだら trickling; sluggish; gently
- 蜂蜜が～(と)蜂の巣から流れ出た honey oozed from the honeycomb. 坂道が～(と)続いた the road continued in a gentle slope. ～(と)仕事をする work sluggishly.
- ～(と)した生活 a leisurely/lazy

ダラダラ　　　　　　　　　　　　　　　　　　　　　　　　　チクリ

life. Ⓒ ～(と)した坂 a gentle slope. ～(と)した態度 a slovenly attitude.
[する] ～する ❶ be sluggish; go slowly; stall. ❷ be relaxed; Ⓒ kill time.

♦ のろのろ

たらっ drooling; slobbering

[Av] ～とよだれを垂らす drool.
[AJ] Ⓐ ～としたポーズ a relaxed pose. Ⓒ ～とした生活 a lazy/sloppy life. ～とした波 a sluggish wave. Ⓒ ～とした雰囲気 a listless mood. Ⓒ ～とした服装 a sloppy dress.
[する] Ⓒ ～とする loiter about; Ⓒ fool around; Ⓒ Ⓓ loaf about.

たんたん [淡々] Ⓐ indifferent

[N] Ⓐ ～たる unconcerned; disinterested; detached; indifferent. Ⓐ ～たる心境 a serene state of mind.

たんたん [坦々] Ⓑ level

[N] Ⓒ ～たる ❶ level; flat; smooth. ❷ peaceful; regular; uneventful.

たんたん [湛々] Ⓐ overflowing

[N] Ⓐ ～たる overflowing; brimming; deep (waters).

だんだん [段々] gradually; steadily

[Av] ～(と)仕事に慣れる gradually get used to one's work. ～(と)明るくなる gradually grow light.

たんまり ample; substantial

[Av] ～(と)儲ける make substantial profits. ～(と)ほうびを貰う receive ample praise. ～(と)せしめる swindle sb out of a lot of money.

♦ たっぷり ♦ どっさり

ち

ちかちか flittering; twinkling

[Av] 町の遠い灯が～(と)瞬いた the towns lights were blinking in the distance.
[する] 対向車のライトで目が～とする my eyes are dazzled by the light of oncoming traffic.

ちくちく prickling; stinging

[Av] 痛烈な言葉で心が～(と)痛む be stung by sb's harsh words. ～(と)愚痴をこぼす complain incessantly.
[する] 棘が刺さって指が～(と)する my finger tickles from the thorn prick.

♦ ちくり

ちくっ stinging; tingling

[Av] 蜂に刺されて腕が～と痛む my arms hurts from the bee sting.

ちくり stinging; biting

[Av] 皮肉な言葉で耳が～と痛む be stung by a sarcastic remark. ～と嫌

味を言う hurt *sb* with one's sarcastic remarks.
♦ ちくちく

ちっ chirp; cluck (one's tongue)
[Av] 雀が〜と鳴く the sparrow chirps. 男が〜と舌打ちをした the man clucked his tongue.

ちびちび little by little; bit by bit
[Av] 金を〜(と)返す return the money bit by bit. 酒を〜(と)飲む sip one's sake. 〜(と)味わう taste a little bit of *sth*. アイスクリームを〜(と)舐める savor one's ice cream.
[N] ⓒ 〜の変化 piecemeal change.

ちまちま small; compact
[Av] 〜(と)書かれた文字 written in a tiny hand.
[Aj] ⓒ 〜とした顔立ちの女 a woman with delicate features. 東京の〜とした生活 Tokyo's cramped living.

ちゃっかり shrewd; cunning
[Av] 猫が〜(と)座布団の上に丸くなった the cat had craftily curled up on my *zabuton* (meditation cushion).
[Aj] 〜(と)した奴 a cunning fellow.

ちゃぽちゃぽ splashing; sloshing
[Av] 〜(と)水溜りを歩く slosh through a puddle. 〜(と)湖に入る enter the lake with a splash. お腹が〜(と)音がした my stomach made a sloshing sound.
♦ じゃぶじゃぶ ♦ ばしゃばしゃ

ちやほや pamper; spoil; fawn
[Av] 子供を〜(と)甘やかす make a fuss over one's child; pamper a child.

ちゃらちゃら jingling; chatty; flirty
[Av] 小銭が〜(と)いっている the coins are jingling (in my pocket). 〜(と)喋る人 a chatty person.
[Aj] 〜(と)した格好 a showy/flashy appearance.
[する] ⓐ 雪駄を〜とさせて歩く make one's sandals flop as one walks.

ちゃらんぽらん sloppy; off-hand
[N] 仕事が〜だ be a sloppy worker. 〜な奴 a slovenly guy. 〜な事を言う make off-handed remarks.

ちゃりん tinkle; jingle; jangle
[Av] 10円玉が〜と落ちてきた the ten-yen coins came jingling (out of the machine). 硬貨が〜と鳴った the coins jingled.
♦ じゃらじゃら ♦ ちりんちりん

ちゃん regular; straight; neatly
[Av] 〜と覚えている remember *sth* precisely. 〜と知っている know

exactly (what is going on). ～と家賃(やちん)を支払(はら)う pay one's rent on time.
[A] ～とした職業(しょくぎょう) a respectable job; a decent occupation. ～とした家(いえ) a respectable family. ～とした生活(せいかつ)を送(おく)る lead an orderly life. ～している人(ひと) be an upright person.

♦ ちゃん

ちゅーちゅー squeaking; chirping

[Av] ～(と)卵(たまご)を吸(す)う suck out an egg. 雀(すずめ)が～(と)鳴(な)く the sparrow chirps.

ちゅっ kissing

[A] ほっぺに～とキスをする kiss sb on the cheek; give sb a peck on the cheek.
[する] ～とする kiss.

ちょいちょい often; lightly

[Av] リスは～(と)枝(えだ)から枝(えだ)へ飛(と)び移(うつ)った the squirrel lightly jumped from one branch to the other. ～(と)彼女(かのじょ)の家(いえ)を訪(たず)ねる frequently visit her house.

ちょうちょう [喋々] [A] chatter

[する] ⓐ ～する chatter; talk glibly; be long-winded.

♦ なんなん [喃々]

ちょきちょき snipping; cutting

[A] ～(と)髪(かみ)の毛(け)を切(き)る snip away at sb's hair. ～(と)新聞(しんぶん)の記事(きじ)を切(き)り抜(ぬ)く cut out a newspaper article.

ちょくちょく often; repeatedly

[Av] ～(と)遊(あそ)びに来(く)る come over regularly to have fun. ～(と)顔(かお)を出(だ)す show one's face regularly.

♦ しばしば ♦ たびたび

ちょこちょこ quickly; restlessly

[Av] ～(と)動(うご)く move constantly. ⓒ ブログを～(と)更新(こうしん)する update one's blog regularly. 子供(こども)が～(と)歩(ある)く the baby toddles about. ～(と)やってのける ① make short work of sth.
[する] ～する be restless; move constantly.

ちょこまか restlessly; in motion

[Av] ～(と)動(うご)き回(まわ)る be constantly on the move. 彼(かれ)は～(と)親(おや)の世話(せわ)を焼(や)いていた he was constantly looking after his parents.
[A] ～(と)した人(ひと) a restless person.
[する] ～する be restless; move constantly.

ちょこん slightly; lightly

[Av] ～とお辞儀(じぎ)する make a little bow. 子供(こども)が～と座(すわ)っていた the child was sitting all by himself. バットを～と当(あ)てる hit a ball lightly (with one's bat).

ちょっきり precisely; exactly

🅰 ◎ ～一万円かかった it cost exactly ten thousand yen. 枝を～(と)切る cut the branch(es) off in one stroke.

ちょっぴり a bit; slightly; just

🅰 ～(と)酒を飲む have a tot of sake. ～(と)悲しかった I was a bit sad. オリーブ油はもう～しかない the olive oil is almost finished.

◆ ぽっちり

ちょぼちょぼ sparsely; equal

🅰 ◎ 庭に～(と)草が生える weeds are coming up around the garden. ◎ 本が～(と)売れている the books are only selling piecemeal.

🅽 ◎ お爺さんの髪は～だ granddad's hair is becoming sparse. ◎ 彼らの成績は～だ their grades were about equal. ◎ 両者の力量は～だ the two of them are matched in strength.

ちょろちょろ trickling; flickering

🅰 ～(と)湧き出る湧き水 a trickling spring. ～(と)燃える炎 a flickering flame. 鼠が～(と)逃げた the mice scampered away.

🆂 ～する dart about; scamper about; move rapidly.

◆ ちろちろ

ちょん clap; chop; poke; dot

🅰 紐を～と切る cut through a string. 拍子木を～と打つ strike wooden clappers together. 鳥が～と彼女の肩に止まった the bird plopped down on her shoulder.

🅽 ⓐ ～の間に before you know it. ⓢ ～になる be cut off; be ended; be over; ⓒ ① get fired. ⓢ 人員整理で～になった I was let go as a result of workforce reductions.

ちらちら glimmering; glimpsing

🅰 噂が～(と)耳に入る get wind of a rumor. 雪が～(と)舞い始める the snow is beginning to whirl (in the wind). 花びらが～(と)散っている the petals are falling to the ground. 怪しい奴が～(と)こっちを見ている a creepy guy is repeatedly glancing this way/at us.

🆂 テレビの画像が～(と)する the television screen flickered.

🆂 人影が～する catch a glimpse of sb.

ちらっ at a glance; by accident

🅰 ～と見る glance at sb/sth. 離婚の噂を～と聞いた I heard (the rumor) of their divorce by accident.

ちらほら sporadically; sparsely

🅰 桜が～(と)咲いている here and

there cherry blossoms are blooming. 髪に白いものが〜(と)混じる there are sprinkles of grey at the temples.

ちりちり sizzle; frizzle; shrivel
[Av] 魚が〜(と)焼けている the fish is sizzling (on the grill). 〜(と)巻く curl up. ⓐ 〜(と)顫える shiver with fear. 〜(と)身が締まる shrivel up. 熱いお風呂が肌を〜(と)刺す the hot bath stimulates my skin.
[Aj] 〜(と)した髪の毛 frizzy hair.

ちりんちりん jingling; ringing
[Av] 風鈴が〜と鳴った the wind chime tinkled. 鈴の〜と鳴る音 the ringing of a (small) bell.

♦ じゃらじゃら ♦ ちゃりん

ちろちろ flicker; trickle; glance
[Av] 炎が〜(と)燃えた the flame flickered. 〜(と)流れている小川 a trickling brook. 蛇が〜(と)舌を出した the snake flicked its tongue.

♦ ちょろちょろ

ちん ding; honk; snort; microwave
[Av] 電子レンジが〜と鳴った the microwave went 'ding.' 〜と鼻をかむ blow one's nose. 鉦を〜と鳴らす sound a hand bell.
[する] ⓒ 〜して食べる食品 microwavable foods.

ちんちろりん chirping; twittering
[Av] 〜と鳴る松虫 a chirping pine cricket. 風鈴が〜と鳴った the wind chime tinkled.

ちんちん chink; ringing; begging
[Av] やかんが〜(と)沸いている the kettle is singing. 鈴が〜(と)鳴った the bell rang.
[する] ⓒ 犬に〜させる make a dog beg (on its hind legs).

ちんちん [沈々] [E] hushed; silent
[N] ⓔ 〜たる夜 a silent night.

♦ しゅくしゅく [肅々]

ちんまり snugly; cosily; compactly
[Av] 〜(と)部屋の隅に座る sit diffidently in the corner of the room.
[Aj] 〜(と)した家 a cozy (little) house. 〜(と)した目鼻立ち charming looks; look cute.

つ

ついつい straight; unintentionally
[Av] ⓐ 霜柱が〜(と)立っている the ice needles stood up straight. 〜言いそびれる forget to tell sb about sth. 〜(と)高いドレスを買ってしまった I couldn't resist buying the expensive dress.

つかつか briskly; determinedly
- Ⓐᵥ ～(と)歩み寄り walk (straight) up to sb. ⓐ 口に任せて～(と)言う speak one's mind.

つくづく deeply; keenly; intently
- Ⓐᵥ 顔を～(と)眺める look intently at sb's face. ～(と)考える think sth over carefully; consider sth carefully. ～(と)感謝する de deeply grateful.
- ♦ しみじみ ♦ じんみり

つけつけ bluntly; frankly; freely
- Ⓐᵥ ⓐ 面と向かって～(と)言う speak one's mind to sb's face. ⓐ 思うことを～(と)言う bluntly say what's on one's mind.

づけづけ bluntly; frankly; freely
- Ⓐᵥ 面と向かって～(と)言う speak one's mind to sb's face. 思うことを～(と)言う bluntly say what's on one's mind.

つだつだ [寸々] Ⓐ torn; shredded
- Ⓐᵥ ⓐ 手紙を～に裂く tear a letter to pieces. ⓐ 服が～に裂けた the dress was all torn up.
- Ⓐᵢ ⓐ 身も心も～だ be broken, both in spirit and in body.
- Ⓝ ⓐ ～になる be cut up; be shredded; be ripped up.
- ♦ ずたずた [寸々]

つぶつぶ [粒々] grainy; lumpy
- Ⓐᵢ ～(と)した食感 (have) a grainy texture/taste; taste lumpy.

つべこべ complaining; nitpicking
- Ⓐᵥ ～言うな stop complaining!
- ♦ くだくだ ♦ ぐだぐだ ♦ くどくど

つやつや [艶々] glossy; slick
- Ⓐᵢ ～(と)した髪 glossy hair. ～(と)した顔色 a glowing complexion.

つるつる slick; slurping; slippery
- Ⓐᵥ そばを～(と)啜る slurp down one's noodles.
- Ⓐᵢ ～(と)した肌 smooth skin. ～(と)した歩道 a slippery sidewalk.
- ♦ ずるずる ♦ すべすべ ♦ のっぺり

つるり smoothly
- Ⓐᵥ 彼は～と滑って転んだ he slipped and fell. ～と禿げ上がった顔 a balding head; a receding hairline.

つん aloof; pungent; pointed
- Ⓐᵥ 匂いが～と鼻をついた the stench assailed the nostrils.
- Ⓐᵢ ～としている be haughty; be stuck up; be standoffish. ～とした鼻 a pointed nose.

つんつん aloof; morose; pungent
- Ⓐᵥ 匂いが～と鼻をついた the stench

ツンツン　　　　　　　　　　　　　　　　　　　　　　　　　　　　　　　デレッ

assailed the nostrils. 魚(さかな)が〜と餌(えさ)を突(つ)いた the fish were snatching up the bait. ⓒ 〜と伸(の)びる茎(くき) the straight corn stalks.

Ⓐ ⓒ 〜している be morose; ⓒ ⓘ be stuck up. ⓒ 〜とした鼻(はな) a pointed nose.

す ⓒ 匂いが〜する have pungent smell; the stench is unbearable.

♦ ぶんぶん ♦ ふわっ

て

ていてい [亭々] Ⓔ Ⓐ lofty; tall
Ⓝ ⓒ ⓐ 〜たる木(き) lofty trees. ⓒ ⓐ 〜たる超高層(ちょうこうそう)ビル towering buildings.

でかでか Ⓒ huge; over the top
Ⓐ ⓒ 事件(じけん)は〜と夕刊(ゆうかん)に報道(ほうどう)された the incident was played up big in the evening papers.
Ⓐ ⓒ 〜としたキャバレ an extravagant cabaret show. ⓒ 〜とした広告(こうこく)キャンペーンを開始(かいし)する launch a huge advertising campaign.

てきぱき briskly; promptly
Ⓐ 仕事(しごと)を〜(と)片付(かたづ)ける get one's work done in no time. 〜(と)動(うご)く move vigorously.
Ⓐ 〜(と)した態度(たいど) a brisk manner. 〜(と)した受(う)け答(こた)え a quick response.

♦ きびきび ♦ すたすた ♦ ぱきぱき

てくてく Ⓒ steadily; trudgingly
Ⓐ 〜(と)歩(ある)き続(つづ)ける trudge along.
♦ とぼとぼ

でこでこ Ⓒ Ⓐ thick; fat
Ⓐ ⓒ ⓐ 〜(に)化粧(けしょう)する apply heavy makeup. ⓒ ⓐ 〜(に)金(かね)を持(も)つ have lots of money. ⓒ ⓐ 〜(と)飾(かざ)り立(た)てる dress sth up gaudily.
♦ こってり

でこぼこ unevenness; bumpiness
Ⓐ 〜した表面(ひょうめん) an uneven surface. 税金(ぜいきん)の〜をならす level/even tax inequalities.
す 〜する be uneven; be bumpy.

でっぷり Ⓒ fat; stout; corpulent
Ⓐ ⓒ 〜(と)肥(こ)える grow fat.
Ⓐ ⓒ 〜(と)した体(からだ)つき be corpulent. ⓒ 〜(と)した紳士(しんし) a gentleman of impressive physique.

てらてら shining; gleaming
Ⓐ 日(ひ)が〜(と)照(て)り出(だ)した the sun burst through (the clouds).
Ⓐ ⓒ 〜(と)したはげ顔(かお) a gleaming bald head.
す 彼女(かのじょ)の顔(かお)が汗(あせ)で〜していた her face was gleaming with sweat.

でれっ Ⓑ slovenly; moonstruck
Ⓐ ⓢ 〜と目尻(めじり)を下(さ)げる ❶ be all

smiles. ❷ ① make eyes at sb; ① give sb the eye.
[する] Ⓐ ⑤ 婦人へ〜とする be lovestruck by a lady.

でれでれ ⑤ lazy; slovenly; flirting
[Av] ⑤ 彼は〜している he looks slovenly; he looks unkempt; ⓒ he's a slob.
[する] ⑤ 女性に〜する dally with a woman; lust after a woman.

でん imposingly; heavily
[Av] 〜と座る sit immovably; 〜と構える stand unflinchingly.

てんてん [転々] ⑥ passing; moving
[Av] ⓒ 〜と努め先を変える frequently change one's employment.
[する] ⓒ 〜とする pass hands many times; go from hand to hand.

と

どーどー roaring; stamping; whoa
[Av] 〜と落ちる滝 a roaring waterfall. 風が森を〜と吹き抜けた the wind roared through the forest.

とうとう [滔々] ⑥ rushing
[N] ⓒ 〜たる川 a rushing river.

どうどう [堂々] ⑥ magnificent
[Av] ⓒ 〜と議論する argue creditably. ⓒ 〜と振る舞う behave in a dignified manner; act gallantly.
[N] ⓒ 〜たる ❶ stately; magnificent; splendid. ❶ fair; square; open.

どーん bang; boom; whump
[Av] 発破の音が〜と谷に響き渡った the sound of the blast reverberated through the valley. 彼が〜とドアに体当たりした he threw himself against his door with all his weight.

どかっ thud; slam; heavily
[Av] 〜と荷物を置く put down one's luggage with a thud. 〜と腰を下ろす plump oneself down. 雪が〜と屋根から落ちた the snow slid from the roof with a thud. お金が〜と入る have a sudden windfall.

♦ がつん ♦ ごつん ♦ ごん ♦ どっか

どかん bang; boom; suddenly
[Av] 大砲が〜と鳴った the guns went off with a bang. 爆発が〜と谷に響いていた the explosion echoed around the valley. ⓒ 地価が〜と跳ね上がった the land prices soared. ⓒ ① the land prices went through the roof. ⓒ 海が〜と深くなった the sea suddenly grew very deep.

♦ がたん ♦ だーん ♦ どん

どきどき throbbing; thumping

[Av] 心臓が〜（と）打つ my heart is pounding; ⓘ have one's heart in one's mouth.

[する] 〜する be exited; ⓘ have butterflies in one's stomach.

♦ ばくばく ♦ はらはら

どぎまぎ flurried; upset; nervous

[Av] 〜（と）返答に窮する be at a loss for an answer.

[する] 突然の知らせで〜する be flurried by the sudden news.

とくとく gurgling; glugging

[Av] 酒が〜（と）徳利から注がれた the sake gurgled out the *tokkuri*.

とくとく [得々] [E] proud; elated

[Aj] ⓔ 〜としている be elated; be self-complacent; ⓘ be on the high ropes. ⓔ 〜として語る relate *sth* in an elated manner; recount *sth* triumphantly.

どくどく copiously; profusely

[Av] 血が〜（と）傷口から流れ出た blood gushed (forth) from the wound.

♦ こんこん [滾々]

とげとげ thorny; bristly; sharp

[Aj] 〜した剛毛 sharp bristles. 〜した

言葉 harsh words.

[する] 〜する get touchy.

♦ いがいが

とことこ trotting; toddling

[Av] ）子供が〜（と）歩く the child toddles along.

とことん thoroughly; the end

[Av] 〜調べる investigate *sth* exhaustively. 〜まで戦う fight to the hilt.

どさくさ [E] bustle; frantic

[Aj] ⓔ 〜している be in a state of confusion; rush around; act frantically.

どさどさ one by one; successively

[Av] 警察が〜（と）スタジアムへ入ってきた the police poured into the stadium. 貨物の箱を〜（と）波止場に投げ込む throw the cargo boxes onto the pier (in rapid succession).

どしっ solid; sound; thorough

[Av] 〜と構える be firmly positioned. 〜と動かず stay put.

[Aj] 〜としたデザイン a solid design.

どしどし rapidly; freely; stomping

[Av] 仕事を〜（と）片付ける get one's work done rapidly. 〜（と）本を読む read one book after the other. 先生に〜（と）質問をする fire a string of ques-

tions at the teacher. 階段を〜(と)降りる stomp down the stairs.
♦ じゃんじゃん ♦ どんどん

どしゃどしゃ rushing; pouring
雨が一晩中〜降り続いた the rain poured down all night.
♦ ざーざー ♦ ざんざん

どしんどしん tramping; clumping
〜(と)歩く walk clomp-clomp. 子供が〜(と)暴れ回った the children romped about (the house).

どすんどすん thud; clump; step
〜(と)歩く stomp around; tread heavily. 〜というくい打ち機 the thud-thud of a pile-driving machine.

どたどた noisily; heavily
廊下を〜(と)歩く walk noisily through the hallway.

どたばた noisily; heavily
〜している be in a state of confusion. 〜(と)歩く walk heavily; pound along. 〜(と)階段を上がる stomp up the stairs.
〜する be noisy; Ⓒ make a din.

どっ burst out; surge; rush
聴衆が〜と笑い出した the audience burst out laughing. 電子メールが〜と入ってきた the e-mails poured in. 〜と床につく suddenly fall ill. 女の子が劇場へ〜と押し寄せた girls thronged the theatre.
♦ とっと

どっか Ⓐ thump; flop; plunk
ⓐ 〜と荷物を置く put down one's luggage with a thud. ⓐ 〜と腰を下ろす plump oneself down. ⓐ 大石を〜と据える place the rock down with a thud.
♦ がつん ♦ ごつん ♦ ごん ♦ どかっ

どっかり plunk; flump; flop
〜(と)椅子に腰を下ろす sink heavily into a chair. 〜(と)椅子に座る flop down on a chair. 売り上げが〜(と)減った sales suddenly slumped. 梅雨前線が〜(と)胡座をかいた the seasonal rain front settled in.

とっくり thoroughly; carefully
ⓐ 〜(と)考えてやる do *sth* after careful consideration. ⓐ 〜(と)相談する discuss *sth* thoroughly.

どっさり heaps; plenty; thud
〜(と)買物をする do lots of shopping; shop till one drops. おみやげを〜(と)貰う receive loads of presents. 〜(と)落ちる land with a thud.
♦ たっぷり ♦ たんまり

どっしり bulky; heavy; dignified

[A] ～(と)した建造物 a massive structure. ～(と)した重い鞄 a heavy suitcase. ～(と)した態度 a dignified manner. ～(と)した城門 imposing castle gates.

♦ ずしっ ♦ ずっしり

とっと [S] quickly; at once

[Av] ⓢ ～と歩く walk quickly; keep up a brisk pace. ⓢ ～と出かけなさい get going! ⓢ ～と消え失せろ ⓢ ① get out of my face!

♦ どっ

とつとつ [訥々] [A] faltering

[A] ⓐ ～と話す stammer.

どっぷり totally; wholly

[Av] 温泉に～(と)漬かる have a long soak in the onsen. 安穏な暮らしに～(と)漬かる live a life immersed in peace and tranquility. 筆に墨を～(と)付ける let one's brush soak up plenty of ink. 悪の道に～(と)漬かる sink into a life of crime.

どてっ large; strapping; hefty

[A] 部屋の真ん中に～と寝そべっている lay sprawled out at the center of the room. ～と引っ繰り返る fall flat on one's back. 急に～と寝転がる suddenly lie down.

どでん [A] heavily; hefty; bulky

[Av] ⓐ ～と仰向けに倒れる fall flat on one's back. ⓐ ～と落ちる land with a thud. ⓐ ～とベッドに横たわる lay down heavily on the bed. ⓓ ～買い越す buy on balance.

どぶん plop; splash

[Av] 彼が～と河に飛び込んだ he plunged into the river with a splash.

♦ ざんぶり ♦ じゃぶん ♦ じゃぼん

とぼとぼ tollering; trudging

[Av] ～(と)歩く trudge along.

♦ てくてく

どぼどぼ glugging; gurgling

[Av] ソースを～(と)豚カツに注ぐ pour loads of sauce on one's *tonkatsu*. コンクリートを(と)注ぎ入れる pour in the concrete.

どやどや noisily; babbling

[Av] ⓒ ～(と)集まる throng together. 人が～(と)会場から出てき来た the people left the assembly hall noisily. ⓒ ～(と)出る pile out.

とろっ syrupy; creamy; dozing

[Av] ～と溶けたチーズ softly molten cheese.
[A] ～と(した)野菜カレー creamy vegetable curry. ⓒ ～としたと思う

feel oneself dozing off. 味噌汁がかなり〜としている be *miso* soup is rather thick.

[する] 〜とする doze/nod off.

どろっ thick; starchy

[A] 〜としたマッシュポテト thick mashed potatoes.

とろとろ dozing; simmer; smolder

[A] 〜(と)煮る simmer. 〜(と)煮込む stew. ⓒ 〜(と)歩く amble along; ⓒ ⓘ loaf about. ⓐ 火が〜(と)燃えている the fire is smoldering.

[N] 〜になる become thick.

[する] 〜する doze/nod off. 仕事を〜する neglect one's work; be slow on the job.

どろどろ muddy; sordid; rumbling

[A] 太鼓が〜(と)鳴って入る the *taiko* are rumbling. 〜(と)流れる溶岩 slowly flowing lava. 雷鳴が遠くで〜(と)轟いた a peel of thunder rumbled in the distance.

[A] 〜(と)した娯楽産業の裏側 the sordid side of the entertainment industry.

[N] 〜になる become mushy.

とろり thick; viscous; drowsy

[A] 〜と溶けたチーズ softly molten cheese. 〜と眠くなる feel drowsy.

[A] 〜としている be drowsy. 〜とした舌触り have a creaminess pleasant to the palette. 〜とした肉汁 thick gravy. ⓒ 〜としたと思う feel oneself dozing off. 〜とした目 drowsy eyes.

どろり thick; muddy; gooey

[A] 蜂蜜が〜と机に垂れていた the honey tricked onto the table. 〜と濁った川 a murky river. 〜と固まる harden into a gooey substance.

とろん drowsy; intoxicated

[A] 〜としている be drowsy. 〜とした目 drowsy eyes.

どろん disappear; slip away; dull

[A] 幽霊が〜と消えた the ghost suddenly disappeared.

[A] 〜とした色 a dull color.

[する] 〜とする slip away unnoticed.

どん bang; boom; slam; very

[A] 大砲が〜と鳴った the gun rang out. 太鼓を〜と打つ hit a *taiko* hard. 車が〜とぶつかった the cars slammed into each other. 〜と金を出す plunk down a wad of money.

♦ がたん ♦ だーん ♦ どかん

とんとん evenly; smoothly

[A] 彼女が窓を〜(と)叩いた she

tapped on the window. 会議が〜（と）進んだ the meeting went smoothly. N 収支が〜になる balance the budget; break even; ⓘ make both ends meet.

どんどん drumming; rapidly
Ⓐ 扉を〜（と）叩く bang on the door. 花火が〜（と）上がった fireworks went up with a bang. ⓒ 〜（と）金を貯める grow rich fast; ⓘ make money hand over fist. 仕事が〜進む make rapid progress with one's work.

♦ じゃんじゃん ♦ どしどし

どんぴしゃり drumming; rapidly
Ⓐ 〜だ be spot-on; hit the mark.

どんより dark; dull; heavy
Ⓐ 〜（と）曇った空 a dark/leaden sky. 〜（と）疲れた feel lackluster.
Ⓐ 〜（と）した日 a dull day; an overcast day. 〜（と）した目つき a dull look. 〜（と）した天気 dull weather.

な

なみなみ to the brim
Ⓐ 酒を〜（と）注ぐ fill (one's glass) to the brim with *sake*.

♦ たっぷり

なよなよ gently; weakly
Ⓐ ⓐ 枝が〜（と）風に揺れる the branches sway gently in the wind.
Ⓐ 〜（と）した子 a delicate child. 〜（と）した腰 a slender waist. 〜（と）した男 an effeminate man.

♦ しなしな

なんなん [喃々] Ⓐ chattering
Ⓐ ⓐ 〜と話す chatter.

♦ ちょうちょう [蝶々]

に

にこにこ smiling; beaming
Ⓐ 〜（と）笑う smile broadly.
する 〜する smile; beam.

にこり smiling
Ⓐ 〜ともしない without even a smile. 〜と笑う crack a smile.

にたにた grinning; smirking
Ⓐ 〜（と）笑う smirk; give a smirk.
する 〜する grin (with dismay).

にちゃにちゃ sticky; gummy
Ⓐ 〜（と）歯につく stick to one's teeth. ガムを〜（と）噛む chomp on one's chewing gum.
Ⓐ ⓢ 〜とした口調で in a persistent tone.
する ⓢ 〜する be sticky; slimy.

にっ grinning; smirking
[Av] 〜と笑う smirk; give a smirk.

にっこり smiling; grinning
[Av] 〜(と)挨拶する greet sb with a broad smile. 〜(と)笑う smile sweetly; beam at sb. 〜(と)微笑む smile kindly at sb.
[擬] 〜(と)する smile; beam. 思わず〜(と)する smile despite oneself.

にゃー mewing; miaow; meow
[Av] 猫が〜と鳴く the cat mewed.

にやにや grinning; smirking
[Av] 意味ありげに〜(と)笑う grin meaningfully; give sb a sinister smirk.
[擬] 〜する grin (to oneself). 〜するな stop smirking!

にやり suggestively; meaningfully
[Av] 〜と笑う flash a (meaningful) grin. 皮肉っぽく〜と笑う smile sardonically.

にゅっ suddenly; abruptly
[Av] 襖の陰から〜と出る appear suddenly from behind the *fusuma*. 煙突が〜と立つ the chimney stand out (from the rest of the buildings). 〜と姿を表す suddenly appear.
♦ ぬっ ♦ ひょっ ♦ ぶい ♦ ふっ

にゅるにゅる wriggling; slithering
[Av] 蛇は〜(と)抜けて逃げた the snake slithered away.
♦ もそもそ

にょきにょき spring up; jump up
[Av] 筍が〜(と)生えた bamboo shoots shot up (one after the other). 高層ビルが〜(と)立った high rise buildings rose up one after the other.

にょっきり stick out; jut out
[Av] 山の頂が雲の上に〜(と)顔を出した the top of the mountain appeared above the clouds; Ⓔ the mountain reared its head above the clouds.

にょろにょろ slithering; sliding
[Av] 蚯蚓が〜(と)這い回った the earthworm slithered around.
♦ しゅるしゅる

にんまり complacent; satisfaction
[Av] 密かに〜(と)ほくそ笑む smile complacently to oneself.

ぬ

ぬくぬく [温々] snugly; easily
[Av] 布団に〜(と)包まっている be snugly wrapped in a *futon*. 〜(と)育つ be raised in comfort; have a protect-

ed childhood; have a carefree childhood. ～(と)暮らす live the easy life; live a cozy life; live in comfort.
[Av] ～(と)した手袋 a snug pair of gloves. ～(と)した炬燵 a comfortable *kotatsu*. ～(と)した雰囲気 a safe atmosphere. ～(と)した気分 a carefree mood. ～(と)した気持ち a free and easy feeling.
[する] 部屋の中が～としてくる the room is getting (real) comfortable.

♦ **おんおん** ♦ **のーのー** ♦ **のほほん**

ぬけぬけ freely; brazenly

[Av] ～としらを切る have the impudence to feign ignorance; brazenly pretend not to know. ～と嘘をつく brazenly tell a lie.

ぬっ suddenly; abruptly

[Av] 物陰から～と現れる appear suddenly from the shadow. 入り口に～と立つ loom suddenly in the doorway. ～と立ち上がる suddenly stand up. 音もなく～と現れる appear without a sound out of nowhere.

♦ **にゅっ** ♦ **ひょっ** ♦ **ぷい** ♦ **ふっ**

ぬめぬめ [滑々] wet; slimy; smooth

[Av] 彼女の唇は～(と)光っていた her lips glistened; her lips were wet and glistening.
[Av] ～(と)した蛞蝓 a slimy slug. ～(と)した床柱 a smooth *tokonoma* post. ～(と)した風呂場 a slippery bathroom.

♦ **ぬるぬる**

ぬらぬら slippery; sluggishly

[Av] ～(と)動く slouch along; slither along. ～(と)輝く glisten/glimmer. ～(と)夜に蠢く幽霊 a night crawling with ghosts.
[Aj] ～としている be slippery.

♦ **ぬるぬる**

ぬらりくらり slippery; lazy

[Av] ～(と)言い逃れる glibly talk oneself out of *sth*. ～(と)一生を送る idle away one's life.
[Aj] ～としている be slippery.
[する] ⓒ ～する wander around (aimlessly); ⓒ ① loaf about.

♦ **のらりくらり**

ぬるぬる slimy; slippery; greasy

[N] ～になる become slimy/slippery. ～を洗い流す wash off the grease.
[Av] ～としている be slippery.

♦ **ぬめぬめ** ♦ **ぬらぬら**

ね

ねちねち sticky; nagging; insistent

[Av] ～(と)歯にくっつく stick to one's

teeth. ～(と)言い続ける keep going on about *sth*; refuse to let *sth* rest. ～(と)口を出す keep nagging *sb* about *sth*. 弁護士が証人を～(と)甚振っていた the lawyer kept pressing the witness (on what he had seen).

A ～(と)した人物 a persistent individual. ～(と)した食感 have a sticky consistency. ～(と)したイジメ persistent bullying.

する ◎ 手が～とする one's hands are sticky.

♦ ねっとり ♦ ねばねば

ねっちり persistent; insistent

Av ◎ ～(と)小言を言う keep lecturing/nagging *sb* about *sth*.
A ～(と)した話ぶり have a nagging way of talking; talk in a nagging way.

ねっとり sticky; viscous

Av 汗で～(と)絡み付く be covered in sweat.
A ～としている be clammy (with perspiration). ～(と)した舌触り have sticky texture; taste slicky.
する ～する be sticky.

♦ ねちねち ♦ ねばねば

ねとねと sticky; gooey; sirupy

A 油が～(と)固まった the oil dried up into a sticky consistency.
A ～(と)している be clammy (with perspiration). ～(と)した物 something sticky.
する ～する be sticky.

♦ ねちねち ♦ ねっとり

ねばねば sticky; gummy; insistent

Av ◎ ～(と)戦う fight doggedly.
A ～(と)した物を踏む step on *sth* sticky. ～(と)した話し方 have a persistent way of talking.
する ～する be sticky.

♦ ねちねち ♦ ねっとり

の

のーのー carefree; free and easy

A ～と遊ぶ play without care. ～と暮らす lead an easy life.
A ～とした気分 a carefree mood.

♦ ぬくぬく ♦ のほほん

のこのこ nonchalantly; brazenly

Av ～(と)彼女の前に行く nonchalantly walk up to a girl. ～(と)パーティーにやってくる brazenly gate-crash at a party.

のしのし heavily; lumbering

Av 関取が～(と)土俵にふみ入った the *sumō* wrestler stepped heavily into the *sumō* ring.

♦ のっしのっし

のそのそ slowly; sluggishly

- 〜（と）歩く walk slowly/sluggishly 熊が〜（と）川に向かった the bear lumbered over to the river.
- ♦ ぐずぐず ♦ のろのろ ♦ もたもた

のたのた idlingly; leisurely

- 羊が〜（と）草を食んでいた the sheep were grazing leisurely. 彼は〜（と）酔っ払って歩いた he toddled about drunkenly.
- 〜する loaf about; wander around (aimlessly).
- ♦ のらのら ♦ ゆっくり

のたりのたり rolling; swelling

- 海は〜と畝っていた the sea rolled/heaved gently.
- 〜とした海 a calm sea; a gently rolling sea.

のっしのっし heavily; lumbering

- 〜（と）歩く walk heavily; lumber. 力士が〜（と）入場した the sumō wrestler entered with heavy strides.
- ♦ のしのし

のっそり ploddingly; stolidly

- レスラーが〜（と）立ち上がった the wrestler rose heavily to his feet. 彼が〜（と）玄関に突っ立ていた he stood stolidly at the front porch.
- ♦ ぐずぐず ♦ のそのそ ♦ のろのろ

のっぺり flat; smooth; blank

- 〜（と）した土地 a flat piece of land. 〜（と）した表情 a blank expression. 〜（と）した顔 an expressionless face.
- ♦ つるつる ♦ のっぺり

のほほん nonchalantly; leisurely

- 〜と暮らす live a carefree life. 〜と日を送る spend one's days in leasure. 時間を〜と過ごす spend (one's) hours in idleness.
- 〜としている remain unconcerned; be without a care.
- ♦ ぬくぬく ♦ のーのー ♦ のんびり

のらくら idly; lazily; aimlessly

- 毎日を〜（と）過ごす idle away one's time; lead an idle life.
- 〜とした男 a lazy fellow; a loafer.
- 〜する loaf about; wander around (aimlessly).
- ♦ のたのた

のらりくらり slippery; evasive

- 〜（と）言い逃れる glibly talk oneself out of sth. 彼は〜（と）記者の質問をかわした he skillfully eluded the journalists' questions.
- 一日〜としている while away the day.
- 〜する wander around (aim-

lessly); ⓒ ① loaf about.
- ぬらりくらり

のろのろ slowly; sluggishly
[Av] ～と歩く slouch along; ① drag one's heels. ～と運転する drive at a snail's pace.
- ぐずぐず - だらだら - もたもた

のんびり carefree; leisurely
[Av] ～(と)暮らす live a carefree life; lead a quiet life. ～(と)旅行する take a leisurely trip.
[Aj] ～(と)した性格 a carefree temperament. ～(と)した経済成長 sluggish economic growth.
[する] ～する relax; take it easy; ⓒ take it slow.
- ぬくぬく - のーのー - のほほん

のんべんだらり idly; sluggishly
[Av] ～と過ごす spend one's time in idleness. ～と日を送る spend one's days in idleness.
[Aj] ～とした暮らし an idle life.
[する] ～とする idle one's time away.

は

ぱーっ all out; enthusiastically
[Av] ⓒ ～とやろう let's do it! ⓒ ① let's get cracking! ～と決める decide on the spot. ⓒ ～と行こう let's go!

はーはー gasping; panting
[Av] 両手に～(と)息を吹きかける warm one's hands with one's breath. ～(と)息を切らす be out of breath; gasp for air.
- えんえん - ぜいぜい - ふーふー

ばーん bam; bang; wham
[Av] 曲がり角で～と彼女にぶつかった I banged into her on the corner. バルーンが～と破裂した the balloon exploded with a bang.

ぱかっ split; tear; snap
[Av] ひな鳥が口を～と避けた the fledgling tore its beak wide open. まな板が～と二つに割れた the cutting board split right in two.

ばきっ whack; crack
[Av] 木が～と折れた the tree broke with a heavy crack.

はきはき briskly; clearly; lucidly
[Av] ～(と)答える give a clear answer; answer promptly. ～(と)物を言う be outspoken. ⓒ ～(と)治らない take a long time to recover.
[Aj] ～(と)した行動 decisive action. 頭が～している be lucid/sharp.

ぱきぱき briskly; crisp; snappy

[A] 小枝を〜(と)切る cut off the twigs briskly (one after the other). 背中の骨が〜(と)鳴った the ligaments in my back made a snapping sound.

[A] ⑤〜(と)した話し振り a snappy way of talking; fire off words in rapid succession.

♦ きびきび ♦ すたすた ♦ てきぱき

ばくばく thumping; pounding

[A] 心臓が〜(と)鳴っていた my heart was pounding. 餃子を〜食べる stuff oneself with gyōza.

[する] 胸が〜する feel one's heart beating fast.

♦ どきどき ♦ はらはら

ばくばく [漠々] [E] vast

[N] ⑤ⓐ〜たる海面 a vast expanse of water. ⓒⓐ〜たる砂漠 the boundless desert.

♦ かいかい [怪々] ♦ まんまん [漫々]

ぱくぱく gasping; munching

[A] ご飯を〜(と)食べる munch away on one's rice; devour one's rice. 口を〜(と)させる gasp (with surprise.

[する] ⑤ 靴が〜する the (torn) shoe gapes open and shut.

ぱくり gaping; snapping; rip-off

[A] 傷口が〜と開いていた the wound was wide open. 鯉が餌を〜と飲み込んだ the carp snapped at the bait.

[N] ⑤ 有名な歌の〜 ⓒ a rip-off of a famous song.

ぱこぱこ typing; plopping

[A] ⑤ インスタグラムを〜(と)更新する make constant updates to one's Instagram account. 〜(と)書き綴る type (heartily) away (at one's computer). ⑤ iPadで〜(と)打つ write on one's iPad; tap away on one's iPad. 〜(と)音が鳴る the sound of tapping/typing.

[する] ⓒ ⑤ 〜する have sex. 〜する蓋 a lid that plops; a floppy lid.

ばさっ rustle; swoosh; flap; flop

[A] 〜と紙のカバンに入れる stuff it all into a paper bag. 投網を〜と広げる cast a net with a swoosh. 髪を〜と切る cut one's hair short.

[A] 〜とした質感 have a loose texture; have a papery texture.

ばさばさ unkempt; rustling; whack

[A] 鳥が羽を〜(と)羽ばたいた the bird flapped its wings with a rustle. 木の葉が〜(と)音を立てた the leaves (on the trees) rustled. 予算を〜(と)削る cut back (decisively) on budget; make (decisive) budget cuts.

バサバサ ハタハタ

A ～とした髪 ❶ have unkempt hair; wear one's hair loose. ❷ dry hair.
N ⑤ ～の髪 ❶ unkempt/loose hair. ❷ dry hair.
♦ ばさり ♦ はたはた ♦ もじゃもじゃ

ぱさぱさ dry; crisp; crumbly
A ～(と)した髪の毛 have dry and dead hair; have dry hair without any gloss. ～(と)したご飯 dry and tasteless rice.
N ～のパン dry and crumbly bread. ～の髪 dry and dead hair.

ばさり thud; flapping; beating
A 鷲が羽を～と羽ばたかせた the eagle beat its wings. テントが大風で～となった the tent flapped in the heavy wind. 太い枝が～と落ちた the thick branch landed with a thud.
♦ ばさばさ ♦ はたはた ♦ もじゃもじゃ

ぱしっ tapping; slapping; snapping
A 彼女が～と平手打ちを食わらわせた she slapped him with the palm of her hand; ⓒ ⓘ she let fly with a slap. と会議を～と打ち切る abruptly end a meeting; break off a meeting.

ばしゃっ splashing; sloshing
A トラックが～と水を跳ねた the truck slashed water all over the place.
♦ じゃぶじゃぶ ♦ ちゃぽちゃぽ

ぱしゃっ splashing; snapping
A 鯉が～と水をはねた the carp leaped with a splash. ～とシャッターを切る press the shutter (with a snap); snap an image.

ばしゃばしゃ splashing; clicking
A 水たまりを～(と)歩く splash through a puddle; walk splash-splash through a puddle. ～(と)雨が降る the rain comes splashing down.
♦ じゃぶじゃぶ ♦ ちゃぽちゃぽ

はた suddenly; fiercely; utterly
A ～と思いつく suddenly thing of sth; hit upon an idea; be struck by a thought. ～と睨む glare/stare hard at sb. ～と忘れる forget all about sth. ～と言葉に詰まる be at a loss what to say; be lost for words.

ばたっ thud; flop; snap
A ～と倒れる suddenly fall over. ～と来なくなる suddenly stop coming.

はたはた fluttering; flapping
A 旗が風に～(と)はためいていた the flag was fluttering in the wind. 帆が～(と)翻った the sail fluttered in the wind. 蝶が羽を～(と)揺らめかせた the butterfly fluttered with its wings.
♦ ばさばさ ♦ ばさり ♦ ひらひら

は

75

ばたばた clattering; trampling

[Av] 廊下を〜(と)歩く trample down the corridor. 鷲が羽を〜と羽ばたかせた the eagle beat its wings. 〜(と)倒れる collapse one after another. ⓒ 伝染病で人が〜(と)死んだ ⓒ people died like flies in the epidemic.
[Aj] 職場が〜(と)している the workplace is in a kerfuffle. 〜街が祭りの準備で〜(と)している the town is astir with preparations for the *matsuri*.
[する] 〜する make a fuss.

♦ ばったばった

ぱたぱた flapping; fluttering

[Av] スリッパの〜(と)いう音 the patter of flip flops. 風に帆が〜(と)音を立てていた The sails fluttered in the wind. 仕事を〜(と)片付ける be quick to one's work. ⓒ 布団を〜(と)払う beat a *futon*; ⓒ whack a *futon*. 〜(と)倒れる topple over like dominoes.
[する] 〜する patter; clatter; flutter.

♦ ばさばさ ♦ ばさり ♦ もじゃもじゃ

ばたん bang; slam; thud; crash

[Av] 〜とドアを閉める slam the door shut. 箪笥が〜と倒れた the wardrobe fell over with a crash.

ぱちくり blinking

[する] 目を〜(と)させる blink one's eyes (in surprise).

ぱちぱち clapping; cracking

[Av] 聴衆が〜(と)手を叩いた the audience clapped their hands. 火が〜(と)燃える the fire crackled. 算盤を〜(と)弾く make calculations on an abacus; click the beads on an abacus. 〜(と)写真を撮る take photographs in quick succession; take one photograph after the another.

ばちゃばちゃ splashing; chubby

[Av] 川の中を〜(と)進んだ (we) made our way splashing through the river; (we) splashed through the river.
[Aj] ⓒ 〜とした手 chubby hands. ⓒ 〜とした子 a chubby child. ⓒ 〜(と)している鳥 a bird washing itself (in water).
[する] 波打際で〜(と)する splash through the water's edge.

♦ ちゃぽちゃぽ ♦ ぽちゃぽちゃ

はっ surprised; quickly; suddenly

[Av] 〜と目がさめる be startled awake. 〜と目を引く instantly draw one's attention. 〜と我に返る (suddenly) come to one's senses. 〜と息を呑む take one's breath away; catch one's breath.
[する] 〜とする be startled; be surprised.

ぱっ suddenly; in a flash; showy

[Av] 噂が〜と広まった ⓘ the rumor

spread like wildfire. ～と駆け出す dash of. ～と体を翻す turn suddenly. ～と見る give *sth* a quick glance.

[する] ～としない don't amount to anything; be unimpressive.

はっきり clearly; plainly; sound

[Av] ～(と)聞こえる hear *sth* clearly. ～(と)言ってくれて良かった thank you for being (so) frank.

[Aj] ～(と)した人 an outspoken person. 中毒の～(と)した症状 clear symptoms of poisoning. ～(と)した返事 a straightforward answer. 原因は～(と)している the cause is clear. お爺さんは頭がまだ～(と)している granddad's mind is still sound.

[する] ～(と)しない天気 unsettled weather. 彼女の病気は～(と)しない she doesn't seem to get any better.

♦ ありあり ♦ くっきり ♦ まざまざ

ばっさり resolutely; drastically

[Av] 予算を～(と)削る drastically cut one's budget; make drastic budget cuts. 枝を～(と)切り落とす lop off a branch; lop off branches.

♦ ざっくり ♦ すっぱり

はっし whack; smack; clack

[Av] ⓒ ～と球を打つ hit the ball hard; ⓒ whack the ball. 刀を～と受け止める parry a sword without fail.

ばったばった mow/cut down

[Av] 敵を機関銃で～となぎ倒す mow down the enemy with a machine gun; machine-gun the enemy.

♦ ばたばた

ばっちり spot on; perfect; plenty

[Av] ⓒ ～(と)稼ぐ ⓒⓘ rake in money. ⓒ ～(と)決まっている ⓘ suit one to a T; ⓒⓘ look a million bucks.

[N] ～だ be spot on; be perfect. ～のロケーション a perfect location.

[する] ～する get it right; spot on; be perfect.

ぱっちり wide open; large

[Av] 目を～(と)開く open one's eyes wide; (stare with) one's eyes wide open.

[Aj] ～(と)した目 bright (wide open) eyes.

はっはっ laughing; panting

[Av] ～と喘ぐ gasp/pant. ～と笑う laugh out loud.

[する] ⓐ ～とする be nervous; ⓘ be on tenterhooks; ⓘ be on needles and pins.

ぱっぱ(っ) puffing; flashing

[Av] ランプが～と点滅する the lamp is flashing. 金～と使う ⓘ spend money like water. 火の粉が～と飛ぶ

sparks went flying (up into the air); the fire sent up sparks.

はつらつ [潑剌] Ⓔ lively; vivid

[Av] Ⓔ ～としている be full of life.
[N] Ⓔ Ⓐ ～たる lively; sprightly; fresh; vivid. Ⓔ Ⓐ ～たる魚 fresh fish. Ⓔ Ⓐ ～たる才気 a keen intellect.

はらはら fluttering; nervous

[Av] 桜の花びらが～(と)舞い落ちた the cherry petals fluttered to the ground. 涙が～(と)落ちた tears poured down (the child's cheeks). 後れ毛が～(と)乱れかかった loose hair was scattered around.
[する] ～する be nervous; ① be on tenterhooks; ① be on needles and pins.

♦ どきどき ♦ ばくばく ♦ はたはた

ばらばら scattered; loose

[Av] 雹が～(と)降った large hail pelted down on us. 武士が～(と)森の中から出てきた warriors came rushing out of the woods in droves.
[Aj] 朝食の時間が～だ breakfast-time is not fixed. 幼児達の動きがまだ～だ the movement of infants is still somewhat uncoordinated.
[N] ～になる break up; become scattered. ～にする take *sth* to pieces; dismantle *sth*. ～の髪 loose hair.

♦ ぼちぼち

ばらばら sparse; crumbly; loose

[Av] 雑誌を～(と)捲る leaf through a magazine. 資料を～(と)見る scan through the data. 山の中に家が～とある among the mountains houses are scattered wide and far between. 崖から小石が～(と)落ちてきた gravel came clattering down from the cliff.

ばりっ tearing; ripping; stylish

[Av] 包み紙を～と破く tear the paper wrapping apart. 窓ガラスに～とヒビが入った the window (suddenly) cracked.
[Aj] Ⓔ ～とした服装 stylish clothing.

ばりっ crispy; crunchy; dashing

[Av] 煎餅を～と噛む crunch a rice cracker with one's teeth.
[Aj] ～とした背広 a dashing business suit.

ばりばり crunching; ripping; stiff

[Av] ～(と)働く work (very) hard. 雑巾は～(と)凍っている the mop is frozen stiff. 漬物を～(と)噛む munch on a pickle. 猫が～(と)襖を引っ掻いた the cat scratched the *fusuma*. 段ボールを～(と)引き裂く tear the cardboard to pieces.
[N] Ⓢ ～のエンジン音 the revving (sound) of an engine; the sound of a

revving engine.
♦ べりべり ♦ べりべり

ぱりぱり crispy; spirited; new

[Av] 瓦が〜(と)砕ける smash the (roof) tiles to pieces. 煎餅を〜と食べる munch on a rice cracker.

[Aj] 〜(と)したお焦げ a crunchy piece of scorched rice.

[N] 〜のお札 a crisp bank note. 〜になった枯れ葉 dried up leaves. 〜の上着 a brand new coat.

ぱん [A] plenty; sufficiently

[Av] ⓢ 煎餅を〜と噛む crunch a rice cracker with one's teeth.

[Aj] ⓐ 〜とした well done; complete.

ぱんぱん bang; hard; fast

[Av] 机を〜(と)叩く hit the desk hard; bang on the desk. 仕事を〜(と)片付ける get one's work done in no time.

ぱんぱん pang; clapping; bursting

[Av] 〜(と)柏手を打つ clap one's hands in prayer (before a shrine). ⓒ ポップコーンが〜(と)弾けた the popcorn popped/burst open.

[N] 〜になる be about to burst. ⓒ 腹が〜だ have a full stomach; have eaten one's fill; ⓒ be stuffed.

ひ

ひーひー shrieking; wailing

[Av] 〜言う cry out (in terror); scream with pain. 赤ん坊が〜(と)泣いていた the baby was screaming.

びーびー screaming; bleating

[Av] 〜(と)悲鳴をあげる scream out in terror. 〜(と)泣く子 a bleating child.

ぴーぴー peeping; hard up

[Av] 〜と鳴る peep.

[Aj] ⓢ 〜だ be destitute. ⓢ 年中〜している eke out a living; ⓘ scrape along.

ぴかぴか sparkle; glitter; glimmer

[Av] 〜(と)光る glitter/sparkle. 〜に磨く polish sth into a shine. 〜(と)瞬く星 a twinkling star.

[Aj] 〜(と)している be shiny.

[N] 〜の靴 ❶ well-polished shoes. ❷ brand-new shoes.

ぴかり brightly; brilliantly

[Av] 稲妻が〜と光った lightning flashed (across the sky).

びくっ jumping; twitching

[Av] 彼女の眉が〜と動いた her eye-

brows twitched.
[する] ～とする be startled; be surprised.

ひくひく twitching; sniff
[する] 鼻を～(と)させる twitch one's nose.

ぴくぴく twitching
[Av] 魚が～(と)動いた the fish was twitching. 彼の頬が～(と)引きつっていた his cheeks were twitching.

びくびく trembling; fearful
[Av] 恐怖で～(と)震える tremble with fear. 彼が～(と)体を動かした he moved timidly.
[AJ] ～(と)している be anxious; ⓘ be on tenterhooks.
[する] ～する be anxious; ⓘ be on tenterhooks.
♦ こわごわ ♦ わなわな

ぴしっ snap; flatly; smartly
[Av] 木の大枝が～と折れた the big branch broke off with a snap. ～と断る refuse sth flatly. ～と叱る tell sb of; scold sb (severely). ～と決める dress smartly.

ぴしっ neatly; tidy; firmly
[Av] 計算が～と合う add up exactly. 鞭を～と鳴らす crack one's whip.

要求を～と撥ね付ける flatly refuse a demand. ～とヒビが入った a crack (suddenly) appeared. ～と決まっている look smart/dashing.
[AJ] ～とした服装 a neat dress.
♦ びしり

ひしひし [粒々] keenly; hard
[Av] 寒さが～と身に染みる the (fierce) cold pierces my body. ～と迫る寒さ a biting cold. 孤独を～と感じる be acutely aware of one's loneliness; feel one's solitude keenly. 大兵が～と城に迫った the large army besieged the castle. ⓐ ～と踏み鳴らす足音 the sound of approaching footsteps.

びしびし stubbornly; relentlessly
[Av] 犬に芸を～(と)教え込む train a dog hard. 竹刀で～(と)打たれる be given a thrashing with the *shinai*. ⓒ 金を～(と)取り立てる extort money relentlessly. 銃弾が～(と)壁に当った bullets struck the wall in rapid succession.
♦ みっちり

ぴしぴし relentlessly; crackling
[Av] 要所を～(と)押さえる thoroughly grasp the main point. 枯れ枝が～(と)爆ぜた the dry twigs were crackling (in the fire). 縁談～(と)断る flatly

turn down a marriage proposal. 鞭を〜(と)鳴らす crack one's whip.

びしゃっ splashing; sloshing
[Av] 卵は〜と潰れた the egg burst on the floor. 〜と血が飛んだ blood went flying (in all directions).

びしゃっ slapping; slamming
[Av] ドアを〜と閉める slam the door shut. 〜と断る refuse sth outright.

びしゃり slapping; slamming
[Av] ⓪ 予想が〜と当たった I guessed exactly right; ⓒ ① I was spot on. 〜と断る refuse sth outright. 〜と平手で引っぱたく slap sb (in the face). 要求を〜と撥ね付ける flatly turn down a demand. 〜と水しぶきが上がった sprays of water went flying. 技を〜と決める execute a technique without wavering.

びしょびしょ soaked; drenched
[Av] 〜と降る雨 drizzling rain. シャツが〜に濡れた (my) shirt got soaked.
[N] 〜になる become soaked/drenched.
♦ ぐしょぐしょ

びしり clicking; snapping
[Av] 鞭を〜と鳴らす crack one's whip. 要求を〜と撥ね付ける flatly refuse a demand. 〜と平手で引っぱたく slap sb (in the face).
♦ びしっ

ひそひそ whispering; secretly
[Av] 〜(と)話す speak in whispers; talk in a low voice. ⓒ 〜(と)陰謀を企む hatch a plot in secret.

ぴたっ tightly; exactly; suddenly
[Av] 平手で頬を〜と打つ slap sb on the cheek. 雨が〜と止んだ the rain suddenly stopped. 〜と言い当てる guess sth right (the first round).

ひたひた lapping; gradually
[Av] 大軍が〜(と)押し寄せてきた the huge army advanced inexorably. 波が〜(と)岸辺を打った the waves lapped at the shore. 波が〜(と)舷を打った the waves rolled against the hull (of the ship). 水を〜に入れる add water until (the vegetables) are just covered. 孤独感が〜(と)胸に迫る thoughts of loneliness came crowding in on me.

ぴたぴた tightly; lightly; patter
[Av] 裸足で〜(と)廊下を歩く patter down the hallway on bare feet. シールを〜(と)貼る stick a seal on tight.

ぴたり tightly; exactly; suddenly
[Av] 計算が〜と合う add up exactly.

先頭に〜と付く be at the head of a vanguard. 酒を〜と止める give up drinking completely. 〜と言い当てる guess *sth* right (the first round). ◎ 意見が〜と一致する be of the exact same mind; ⓒ ① be exactly on the same page. 新幹線のドアが〜と目の前で止まった the door of the *shinkansen* stopped right in front of me. 〜（と）母にくっつく cling to one's mother.

ぴちぴち bursting; splattering

[Av] 〜（と）火花が飛び出た sparks went flying. 〜（と）跳ねる魚 jumping fish. ウイスキーの中の氷が〜（と）音を立てた the ice in the whisky made a crackling sound. 鉄板の油が〜（と）跳ねた the oil spits/spatters on the *teppan* plate.

[Aj] 〜（と）した娘 a lively (young) daughter. 〜（と）した鯉 jumping carp.

[N] 〜のTシャツ a tight-fitting T-shirt. 〜の太もも bulging buttocks.

♦ ぴんぴん ♦ ぽちぽち

びちゃびちゃ splashing; dabbling

[Av] 水溜りを〜（と）歩く slosh through a puddle. ⓐ 〜（と）負ける suffer a crushing defeat.

[Aj] 〜（と）した雑巾 a drenched mop.

[N] 雨で靴が〜になった my shoes became drenched with the rain.

♦ ちゃぽちゃぽ ♦ ぽちゃぽちゃ

ぴちゃぴちゃ smack; slurp

[Av] 犬が〜（と）水を飲んだ the dog lapped up the water. 顔を〜（と）叩く slap *sb's* face (repeatedly). 波が〜（と）舷を打った the waves lapped against the hull (of the ship). 〜（と）舌打ちをする smack one's lips.

ぴっ blow; rip; tear

[Av] 〜と笛を鳴らす blow on a flute. 〜とラベルを剥がす tear off a label.

びっくり startled; surprised; jump

[する] 〜する be startled; be amazed; be surprised. 〜した! you frightened me!

♦ ぎくり ♦ ぎっくり

びっしょり soaking; drenched

[Av] 〜（と）汗を搔く sweat all over; ⓒ perspire profusely.

[Aj] 〜だ be soaking wet; be drenched.

[N] 雨で靴が〜になった my shoes became drenched with the rain.

♦ ぐっしょり

びっしり closely; tightly; densely

[Av] 店が〜（と）建ち並んでいる the shops are crowded close together. 着物を〜（と）箱に詰める stuff the kimonos into a box. 日程は〜（と）詰

まっていた the day's program was jam-packed.
♦ ぎっしり ♦ ぎゅーぎゅー

ひっそり quietly; silently
[A] ～(と)立っている stand (there) all alone. ～(と)暮らす live a secluded life.
[A] ～(と)している be quiet. ～(と)した森 a quiet forest.
♦ こそこそ ♦ こっそり

ぴったし [G] exactly; perfectly
[Av] ⓒ 襖を～(と)閉める close the *fusuma* tightly. ⓒ ～(と)合う fit perfectly. ⓒ 酒を～(と)止める give up drinking completely.
[A] ⓒ ～だ be *just* the right thing. ⓒ ～としたズボン tight fitting pants.
♦ かっちり ♦ きっかり

ぴったり tightly; closely; snugly
[Av] 障子を～(と)閉める close the *shōji* tightly. 酒を～(と)止める give up drinking completely. ～(と)合う fit perfcctly.
[A] ～(と)したズボン tight fitting pants. ～だ be *just* the right thing. ～した言葉 the right/fitting words.
♦ かっちり ♦ きっかり

ぴっちり tightly; snugly
[Av] ～(と)包む wrap *sth* up tightly.

～(と)蓋をする fit a lid on tightly.
[A] ～(と)したドレス a tight-fitting dress.

ひひ(ー)ん neighing
[Av] 馬が～(と)鳴いていた the horses were neighing.

ひやひや [冷々] chilly; nervous
[Av] 雨が～(と)襟首に入った the (cold) rain ran into the back of my neck (and caused me to shiver).
[A] ～(と)している be chilly.
[する] ～する ❶ shudder (with the cold). ❷ be afraid; be rattled.

ぴゅーぴゅー whistling; howling
[Av] 風が隙間から～吹き込んだ the wind howled through the cracks.

ぴゅっ hiss; spit; whistle
[Av] ～と鞭を打ち鳴らす make one's whip cut through the air. ～と口笛を吹く whistle with one's lips. 蒸気が～と筒から吹き出した the steam burst forth from the pipe.

ひゅるひゅる whishing; swishing
[Av] 砲弾は頭上高く～(と)通過した the artillery shells passed high over out heads. 縄が～(と)飛んで行った the rope sailed through the air.

びゅんびゅん swishing; whirling

[Av] 〜(と)刀を振り回す swish a sword through the air. 新幹線が〜(と)風を切った the shinkansen cut through the air.

ひょいひょい lightly; casually

[Av] 〜(と)草の上を跳ねている蝗 a grasshopper hopping about in the grass. Ⓢ 〜(と)冗談を言う casually tell a joke. 何でも〜(と)引き受ける take everything in one's stride.

ひょうひょう [飄々] Ⓔ buoyantly

[Aj] Ⓔ 〜としている be somewhat aloof from the world. Ⓔ 〜とした人 a light-hearted person; an easy-going person.

ひょうびょう [縹渺] Ⓔ haziness

[N] Ⓔ Ⓐ 〜たる ❶ misty; hazy. ❷ vast; limitless. Ⓔ Ⓐ 〜たる山 mountains in the mist; misty mountains. Ⓔ Ⓐ 〜たる海面 a vast expanse of water.

びょうびょう [渺々] Ⓔ boundless

[N] Ⓔ Ⓐ 〜たる大洋 the vast ocean.

びょうぼう [渺茫] Ⓔ limitless

[N] Ⓔ Ⓐ 〜たる海原 the vast ocean.

ひょこひょこ unsteady; bobbing

[Av] 〜(と)歩く walk unsteadily; totter about. 〜(と)出かける take/dash off on the spur of the moment. 頭を〜(と)げる bob one's head (up and down). 〜(と)波に揉まれる bobbing up and down in the waves.

ぴょこん quickly; bouncing

[Av] 〜と頭を下げる nod one's head to/at sb; make a slight bow to sb. 兎が〜と草から飛び出した a rabbit suddenly jumped out of the grass.

ひょっ perhaps; unintentionally

[Av] Ⓒ 〜と思い出す suddenly think of sth; hit upon sth; Ⓒ flash into one's mind. 〜と口に出す say sth out of the blue. Ⓐ 〜と立ち上がる suddenly get up. 〜と外に出る suddenly rush/dash outside.

[する] 〜とすると perhaps; possibly. 〜として by any/some chance; should it happen.

♦にゅっ ♦ぬっ ♦ぶい ♦ふっ

ひょっこり suddenly; abruptly

[Av] Ⓒ 〜と訪ねて来る pay an unexpected visit; Ⓒ show up out of nowhere. Ⓒ 〜と現れる appear suddenly. Ⓒ 〜と思い出す suddenly think of sth; hit upon sth; Ⓒ flash into one's mind.

ひよひよ cheep; tweet; gently

[A] ～(と)鳴く雛鳥 cheeping chicks. ◎ 脈拍で～(と)動く move slightly with each pulse.

[する] ～◎する be frightened; be afraid.

ひょろひょろ tottering; staggering

[A] ◎ ～(と)歩く totter; walk unsteadily. ◎ ～(と)立ち上がる stagger to one's feet. ～(と)伸びる grow tall and thin. ◎ ～(と)後ろに下がる stagger backward.

[A] ～(と)した草 tall grass. ～(と)した青年 a tall and lanky youth.

[する] ⑤ ～する stagger; totter; reel.

ぴょんぴょん hopping; skipping

[A] 蛙が～(と)葉から葉へと飛び移った the frog leaped from one leaf to another. 兎が～(と)跳ねる the rabbit hops around.

ひらひら fluttering; flickering

[A] ～(と)舞い落ちる花びら petals fluttering to the ground. ～(と)飛ぶ蝶 fluttering butterflies.

[する] ～(と)する flutter; flap; flit.

♦ はたはた ♦ はらはら

ひらり nimbly; lightly; swiftly

[A] 彼は～と体をかわした he nimbly dodged (the blow). 彼は～と柵を飛び越えた she nimbly jumped over the fence. ～と刀を抜く swiftly draw one's sword.

ひりひり stinging; smarting

[A] ～(と)痛む smart; sting; burn.

[する] ～する smart; sting; burn.

びりびり ripping; tearing; rattling

[A] 封筒を～(と)破り開く tear open an envelope. 窓グラスが～(と)震えた the windowpanes rattled. 手紙を～(と)裂く tear up a letter. ～(と)きた have an electric shock. 寒さで～(と)痺れる shiver with the cold. この段階ですでに緊張感が～(と)伝わってきた by this time the tension had already risen. ◎ ～(と)痛む ◎ hurt like hell.

[A] ～(と)した感覚 a shocking sensation. ～(と)した痛み a flashing pain. ～(と)した痺れ a tingling numbness.

[する] ⓐ 女に～する be intoxicated with women; lust for women. ⓐ 酒に～する be given to drinking.

♦ ばりばり ♦ べりべり

ぴりぴり burning; stinging

[A] 警察は～している the police is on tenterhooks. 手紙を～(と)引き裂く tear up a letter. 計器の針が～(と)震えた the instrument's needle trembled. 笛が～(と)鳴った the whistle blew.

ピリピリ / フー

する ~する smart; sting; burn. 舌が~(と)する辛さ a spiciness that makes your tongue burn.

ぴん tense; taut; erect; burst
A 計器の針が~と上がった the instrument's needle shot up. 背筋を~と伸ばす stand up straight. 耳を~と立てる prick up one's ears. 綱を~と張る pull a rope taut. その説明は~とこない that explanation didn't make (any) sense. すぐに~ときた it immediately made sense.

ひんぴん [頻々] frequently
A Ⓐ ~と起きる occur frequently.
♦ しげしげ ♦ 繁々 ♦ たびたび [度々]

ぴんぴん hard; throbbing; blaring
A 音楽が~(と)響いた the music was blaring. ◎ 彼女の言葉が~(と)胸に響いた her words touched me; ◎ ① her words hit home. Ⓥ ~(と)勃起する Ⓥ have a massive erection.
する 嫌な予感が~する have an eerie premonition; be filled with dread.

ぴんぴん lively; energetic; grating
A 髪が~(と)立っている my hair is standing up. ~(と)跳ねる魚 jumping fish. ◎ ~(と)心に伝わる feel sth keenly; ◎ ① hit home hard.
A ◎ ~している be full of life/zest;

be in good health; ◎ ① be alive and kicking.
する ◎ ~する be aloof; be disconcerted; be prim.
♦ ぴちぴち

ひんやり chilly; cool; cold
A ~(と)した風 a cool wind.
する 木陰で~する feel cool in the shade of the trees.
♦ しん ♦ ぞくぞく

ふ

ぷい abruptly; suddenly
A 彼は~と会社を辞めた he suddenly quit his job. 彼女は~と横を向いてしまった she abruptly turned her head away (in disapproval). 彼は演奏の最中に~と席を立って出た he suddenly stood up in the middle of the performance and left.
♦ にゅっ ♦ ぬっ ♦ ひょっ ♦ ふっ

ふー puff; huff; sigh; faint
A ~と匙の中の物を吹く blow on one's spoon. ~と息をつく breathe a sigh (of relief). ~と煙を吹く blow a puff of smoke. ~と気が遠くなった feel faint/woozy. 猫が~と毛を逆立った the cat hissed as its hairs stood on end. 彼の影が~と幻のように現

れた his shape appeared out of nowhere like an apparition.

ぷー toot; honk; poof; fart
[Av] 警笛を〜と鳴らす give a blast on one's (car) horn. 〜と頬っぺたを膨らませる puff up one's cheeks.

ふーふー blowing; breathing
[Av] 熱い汁を〜(と)吹く blow on one's hot soup. 〜(と)喘ぐ gasp for air. 〜(と)吹いて火を起こす blow life into a fire. 仕事で〜(と)言う groan under one's work load. 猫が〜(と)鳴く the cat hisses.
[N] ⓒ皆が〜だ ⓒ everyone is knackered/ done in.
[する] 〜する blow (on one's food).
♦ えんえん ♦ ぜいぜい ♦ はーはー

ふかふか soft; fluffy
[Aj] 〜(と)した布団 a soft and fluffy futon. 出来立ての〜(と)したパン freshly baked soft bread. 〜(と)した感触 a soft texture.
♦ くにゃくにゃ ♦ ふわふわ

ふがふが muffled; mumbling
[Av] ⓒ〜言う mumble.
[N] ⓒ〜の声 a muffled voice.
[する] 〜して聞き取れない be hard to follow because of one's mumbling.

ぶかぶか baggy; bulging; warping
[Av] ラッパを〜鳴らす blow hard on a horn.
[Aj] 〜(と)したズボン baggy trousers.
[N] このスカートは〜だ this skirt is too big for me.
[する] 〜する warp; bulge. 漆喰の壁が〜してきた the stuccoed wall had become warped and flaky.
♦ だぶだぶ

ぷかぷか lightly; puffing; tooting
[Av] 煙草を〜(と)吹かす puff away on one's cigarette. ゴミが〜(と)波に揉まれる the rubbish was bobbing up and down on the waves. ラッパを〜鳴らす blow hard on a horn.
♦ すぱすぱ

ぷかり(ぷかり) puffing; bobbing
[Av] 葉巻を〜(と)吹かす puff away on one's cigarette. ブイが〜と波間に浮かんでいた the buoy bobbed up and down in the waves.
♦ ぽかり

ふくいく [馥郁] E fragrant
[N] Ⓔ Ⓐ〜たる花 fragrant flowers.

ぷくっ puffed up; swelling
[Av] 頬っぺたを〜と膨らませる puff up one's cheeks. 蜂に刺された指が〜と腫れた the finger (that had

been) stung by a bee swelled up.
- ♦ ぶっ

ぶくぶく bulging; bubbling

[Av] 〜(と)泡を立てる create bubbles; make foam. 船が見る間に〜(と)沈んだ the boat sank before my eyes. 〜に太った子供 a fat child. Ⓐ 〜(と)呟く mutter *sth* through one's teeth. 〜(と)塩水で嗽する gurgle with salt water; rinse one's mouth with salt water. 〜(と)着膨れする be padded with several layers of clothing.

ぶくぶく bubbly; chubby; cute

[Av] 〜(と)膨らむ be chubby. 〜(と)泡立つ make bubbles.
[Aj] 〜(と)した赤ちゃん a (healthy) chubby baby.
- ♦ ぽっちゃり ♦ むっつり

ふさふさ [房々] bushy; tufty

[Av] 彼女の髪が〜(と)肩に垂れる her abundant hair touches her shoulders. アサツキが〜(と)生えている chives are growing rampantly.
[Aj] 〜(と)した髭 a thick beard.

ぶすっ plunging; glumly

[Av] 彼は〜と横を向いた he looked away sulkily. 彼は短刀を〜と腹に刺した he plunged the dagger into his stomach.

[Aj] 〜とした顔つき a sullen expression; a glum/sulky face.
- ♦ ぶすり

ぶすぶす smoldering; muttering

[Av] 〜(と)文句を言う mutter one's complaints; grumble about *sth*. 火が〜(と)燻る the fire is smoldering. 武士が槍を〜(と)敵の胸に突き刺した the warrior thrust a lance in the enemy's chest repeatedly.
- ♦ ごにょごにょ ♦ ぼそぼそ

ぶすぶす sputtering; pricking

[Av] 火が〜(と)燻る the fire is sputtering. 指先で〜(と)障子に穴を開ける prick several holes into a *shōji* with one's finger.

ぶすり thrusting; glumly

[Av] 〜と刀を腹に突き立てる thrust a sword into *sb's* abdomen.
[Aj] 〜とした顔つき a sullen expression; a glum/sulky face.
- ♦ ぶすっ ♦ むっつり

ふっ suddenly; whiff; puff

[Av] 〜と目が覚める wake up with a start; suddenly wake up. 蝋燭の火を〜と吹き消す blow out a candle's flame. Ⓒ 〜と思い付く suddenly think of *sth*; Ⓒ flash into one's mind.
- ♦ にゅっ ♦ ぬっ ♦ ひょっ ♦ ぷい

ふっ blowing; spitting

[Av] ～と笑い出す burst out laughing. ～と頬っぺたを膨らませる puff up one's cheeks.

♦ ぷくっ

ぶつくさ moaning; complaining

[Av] いつも～言っている always moan about *sth*; complain incessantly. ～言うな stop moaning! stop whining!

ふっくら fully; fluffy; plump

[Av] ～(と)出来上がったパン softly done bread. 鰻を～(と)焼き上げる roast an eel until it is nice and tender. ～(と)仕上がった鶏肉 softly done chicken meat.

[Aj] ～(と)した布団 a fluffy *futon*. ～(と)した頬っぺた puffed up cheeks; full/round cheeks.

ふっつり breaking; snapping

[Av] 細い糸が～(と)切れた the thin thread snapped. 夏が～(と)終わった summer had suddenly ended. ～(と)興味を失う suddenly lose interest. ～(と)姿を見せなくなる stop showing up all of a sudden.

♦ ぽっくり ♦ ぽきっ

ぷっつり snapping; suddenly

[Av] ギターの弦が～(と)切れた the guitar string snapped. ～(と)思い切った I made up my mind there and then. ～(と)興味を失う suddenly lose interest. ～(と)もおっしゃりません I won't tell you anything.

ふっふっ snicker; snigger; titter

[Av] 彼女は～と含み笑った she chuckled to herself.

ふつふつ [沸々] bubbling; boiling

[Av] ～と煮る boil briskly.

ぶつぶつ grunting; bubbling

[Av] ～(と)独り言を言う mutter *sth* to oneself. 呉汁が～(と)煮えている the bean soup was bubbling away. 肌に～(と)湿疹が出ていた eczema erupted on his skin. 障子に～(と)穴を開ける prick holes into the *shōji*.

♦ うずうず ♦ むずむず

ぷつぷつ snapping; knobbly

[Av] ～(と)呟く mutter *sth* (to oneself). 茹でた蕎麦が～(と)千切れた the boiled *soba* broke into bits. 針で～(と)葉書に穴をあける punch holes into a postcard with a needle.

[Aj] ～(と)した膨らみ a knobbly swelling. ～(と)した舌触りの餅 rice cakes with a granular texture.

ふにゃふにゃ limp; soft; mumbling

[Av] ～(と)倒れる collapse; go limp.

[Av] 〜(と)座り込む drop into a crouch. 〜(と)手を振る limply wave one's hand. 〜(と)ぼやいた独り言 words mumbled/muttered to oneself.

[Aj] 〜したやつ a weak guy.

[N] 〜になる go limp; become flabby.

♦ ぐにゃぐにゃ

ぶよぶよ soft; flabby

[Av] 〜と太る grow fat and flabby.

[Aj] 〜(と)したバナナ a soft/mushy banana. 〜(と)した筋肉 flabby muscles. 〜(と)した食感 a soft texture; have a soft bite.

♦ だぶだぶ

ふらっ aimlessly; on a whim

[Av] 〜と倒れる feel dizzy and collapse. 〜と友達を訪れる visit a friend on a whim.

[N] 〜となる grow dizzy; suddenly feel dizzy.

♦ くらくら ♦ くらっ ♦ ふらり

ふらふら unsteady; wavering

[Av] 〜(と)立ち上がる stagger to one's feet. 〜(と)座り込む drop into a crouch. 〜(と)歩く walk unsteadily. 〜(と)庭に出る wander into the garden.

[N] 〜になる become unsteady on one's feet; grow faint.

[する] 〜する ❶ feel light-headed; feel giddy; be unsteady on one's feet. ❷ flap; sway; swing; hang loose. ❸ be undecided; be wishy-washy.

♦ がくがく ♦ ぐらぐら

ぶらぶら swaying; rambling

[Av] 竹の茎が風で〜(と)揺れている the bamboo stalks are swaying in the wind. 〜(と)歩く wander/stroll around (a store). 〜(と)暮らす idle one's life away.

[Aj] 〜している ❶ stroll about; wander around (aimlessly). ❷ be out of work; lead an idle/aimless life.

[する] 足を〜させる dangle one's legs (from the side of the pool).

♦ ぶらり ♦ ぼけっ

ふらり aimlessly; swaying

[Av] 〜とキオスクに立ち寄る wander into a kiosk. 〜と旅に出る set out on an unplanned trip. 〜と映画館に行ってみよう let's go to the music hall (and see what is playing).

♦ くらくら ♦ くらっ ♦ ふらっ

ぶらり dangling; swaying; idly

[Av] 〜と立ち寄る pay *sb* an unexpected visit. 夏休みを〜と過ごす idle away one's summer holiday.

[Aj] 〜としている be out of work; lead an idle/aimless life.

♦ ぶらぶら ♦ ぼけっ

ぷりぷり angry; tender; plump
- A ～(と)怒る get angry; get into a huff.
- A ～(と)した食感 be tender (to taste). ～(と)した歯応え have a tender bite. ～(と)した肌 a plump body.

ぶるぶる trembling; shivering
- A 恐怖で～と震える tremble with fear. 膜が～(と)震動し始めた the membrane began to vibrate.
- する 寒さで～する shiver with cold.

ぶわ(ー)っ floating; drifting
- A ～と浮いている float gently on the surface. 風船が～とに運ばれてしまった the balloon was gently carried away by the wind.
- A ～とした新しい布団 a fluffy new futon.

ふわふわ lightly; fluffy; fickly
- A ～(と)飛ぶ羽毛 softly floating feathers. 白雲が～(と)浮かんで行った the white clouds drifted by. 花粉が～(と)降って来た the pollen came floating down (from the trees).
- A ～(と)した布団 a soft and fluffy futon. ～(と)したケーキ soft/spongy cake. ～(と)した毛並みの猫 a cat with a soft coat.
- ♦ ふかふか

ぶわぶわ spongy; mushy
- A ～(と)膨らむ swell up.
- A ～(と)した紙 mushy paper.
- N ⓒ ～になる become spongy.

ふわり softly; lightly; gently
- A ～と落ちる雪片 softly falling snow flakes. ～と香る茶葉 lightly fragrant tea leaves. 埃は～と飛び上がった the dust rose softly. ～と浴衣を羽織る put on a *yukata* with a light air.
- A ～とした食感 have a soft bite.
- ♦ ふんわり

ふんふん sniff-sniff; uh-huh
- A 彼は～と上の空で聞いた he uh-huhed as he listened (to my story) absentmindedly. ～と相づちを打つ chime in with an approving 'uh-huh.' 相手言うことを～と何でも聞く utter an approving 'uh-huh' at everything sb says.

ふんぶん [紛々] E confusedly
- A ⓒ ⓐ 諸説が～としている differ in opinion; be undecided on a matter; ⓔ have a diversity of opinion.

ぶんぶん buzzing; humming
- A 凧は強い風で～(と)鳴っていた the kite buzzed in the strong wind. 蜂は～(と)耳元を飛んでいる a bee

is buzzing round my ear. エンジンは〜(と)回っている the engine is purring (nicely).

♦ ぎゅんぎゅん

ぷんぷん pungent; fuming

[A] 〜(と)怒る fume/rage at *sth*; be mad at *sb*.

[する] 〜する ❶ stink; reek; rot; smell. ❷ reek of *sth*; be fishy. ❸ fume at *sth*; be angry with *sth*. 卒業制作的匂いが〜(と)する be a cliche graduate work. 犯罪の匂いが〜(と)する reek of crime; have all the hallmarks of a crime.

♦ つんつん ♦ ふわっ

ふんわり airily; fluffily; gently

[A] 〜と落ちる雪片 softly falling snow flakes. 〜と香る茶葉 lightly fragrant tea leaves.

[AJ] 〜(と)した布団 a soft and fluffy *futon*. 〜(と)した食感 a soft texture.

♦ ふわり

へ

ぺこぺこ hungry; fawning; dented

[A] 空き缶が〜(と)凹んだ the tin can caved in with a crunch.

[する] 〜する ❶ bow one's head repeatedly. ❷ fawn; kowtow; bow and scrape. ❸ be starving; be famished.

♦ ぼこぼこ

ぺしゃり squashed; flattened

[A] 小屋は〜と潰れた the hovels were flattened. 卵は〜と潰れた the egg went splat.

♦ ぐしゃり ♦ ぺちゃんこ

へたへた collapsing; flopping

[A] 彼女は〜と道端に座り込んだ she collapsed along the side of the road.

♦ ごろり

べたべた sticky; clinging

[A] 〜とペンキを塗る daub paint (on a canvas).

[A] 汗で〜(と)したシャツ a shirt clinging with perspiration.

[する] 〜する cling to *sth*; stick to each other; be sticky.

ぺたぺた stamping; slapping

[A] 頬っぺたを〜(と)叩く pat *sb* on the cheek. 〜(と)判子を押す stamp *sth* with a seal. 廊下を素足で〜(と)歩く walk sloppingly down the corridor in one's bare feet. 壁に〜(と)ビラを貼り付ける slap a placard on the wall.

♦ ぺちゃぺちゃ

ぺたり slapping; flopping

[Av] 椅子に〜と座る flop down in a chair. 〜と印判を押す stamp sth with a seal. 切手を〜と貼る stick a postage stamp on (a letter).

ぺたん slapping; flopping

[Av] 畳に〜と座る plop down on the tatami mats. 判子を〜と押す stamp sth with a seal.

ぺちゃくちゃ chattering; prattling

[Av] 〜(と)しゃべる prattle on about sth.

ぺちゃぺちゃ prattling; messy

[Av] ご飯が〜(と)炊けてしまった the rice came out mushy.
[N] 〜になる become mushy/gooey.
[する] 〜する be sticky; be gooey.

ぺちゃぺちゃ lapping; smacking

[Av] 〜(と)音を立てる smack one's lips. 〜(と)しゃべる prattle on about sth. 頬っぺたを平手で〜(と)張る slap sb's cheeks with the palm of one's hand.
[する] 〜する slurp one's food.

♦ ぺたぺた

ぺちゃんこ flattened; squashed

[N] 〜になる ❶ be flattened; be crushed. ❷ be at a (complete) loss what to do. タイヤが〜になった the tire was flattened. 家が地震で〜になった the house was flattened by the earthquake.

♦ ぐしゃり ♦ ぺしゃり

べったり sticking; clinging

[Av] 泥が〜(と)靴についている the mud is sticking to the shoes; the shoes are covered in mud. 母に〜(と)くっ付く cling to one's mother.

べっとり sticky; gummy

[Av] ⓢ 〜(と)座っている cling to one's seat; stay put. 汚れが〜(と)機械についている dirt is sticking to the machine. 汗で濡れたシャツが〜(と)体にくっつく the shirt drenched with sweat stuck to his body.
[Aj] 〜(と)したソース sticky sauce.

へっへっ(へっ) hehehe

[Av] 彼は〜と笑った be laughed smugly. 〜と薄ら笑いをする he laughed with a scorning chuckle.

へとへと exhausted; knackered

[N] もう〜だ I'm done in; I'm knackered. 〜になる become tired; get exhausted.

♦ くたくた ♦ ぐったり

べとべと sticky; gooey

[Av] 油で〜(と)する be sticky with oil.

[Aj] ～(と)したガム sticky chewing gum. ～だ be sticky; be gooey.

へなへな weakly; helplessly

[Av] ～(と)座り込む sit down feebly. ～(と)腰を抜かす collapse (into a fit of laughter). 植物が～(と)萎れてしまった the shrubs wilted.
[Aj] ～(と)した合板 a flimsy piece of plywood. ～(と)した男 a weak fellow; a spineless guy. ⓒ ～(と)した生活を送る lead a irresolute life.
[N] ～になる become weak/flimsy.

へべれけ [A] drunk; intoxicated

[Av] ⓐ ～に酔う be drunk; be intoxicated.
[N] ⓐ ～になる become drunk; become intoxicated.
◆ ぐでんぐでん ◆ べろべろ ◆ めろめろ

へらへら foolishly; flippant; thin

[Av] ～(と)笑い出す have a fit of giggles. ⓒ ～(と)燃え上がる burst into flame. ～(と)笑う laugh foolishly.
[Aj] ～(と)した布 fragile cloth. ⓒ ～した奴 a flippant bloke.
 ⓢ ～する be indiscreet; be flippant; act frivolously.
◆ くすくす ◆ くつくつ ◆ めらめら

ぺらぺら non-stop; thin; leisurely

[Av] ～(と)捲し立てる talk without thinking; talk like an idiot; ramble on. ～(と)喋る chatter away; prattle on (about sth).
[Aj] ～(と)した切れ地 flimsy fabric.

ぺらぺら fluently; flipping; thin

[Av] ～しゃべる chatter; gabble; patter. 秘密を～としゃべってしまう ⓒ spill a secret. 本を～(と)捲る leaf through a book quickly.
[Aj] ～だ be fluent (in Spanish).
[N] ～の紙 thin paper. ～のスカート a flimsy skirt. ⓒ ～になる become fluent.

べりべり non-stop; tearing

[Av] ⓢ ～(と)喋る chatter away; prattle on (about sth). 傘は突風で～(と)裂けた the umbrellar was torn by a gust of wind. シールを～(と)剥がす tear off a seal.

ぺろっ stick out one's tongue

[Av] ～と舌を出す stick out one's tongue (at sb). ～と唇を舐める lick one's lips. ⓒ 食事を～と平らげる ⓒ eat one's meal in one fell swoop.
◆ ぺろり

べろべろ drunk; licking

[Av] ⓢ ～に酔っ払う be dead drunk; be plastered. 犬が～皿を舐めた the dog licked the plate clean.

ぺろぺろ licking

[Av] ～と皿を舐める lick one's plate (clean). 食事を～と平らげる ⓒ eat one's meal in one fell swoop. Ⓐ ～と燃え上がる火 licking flames.

ぺろり stick out one's tongue

[Av] ～と舌を出す stick out one's tongue (at *sb*). ～と唇を舐める lick one's lips. ⓒ 食事を～と平らげる ⓒ eat one's meal in one fell swoop.

♦ ぺろっ

へんぺん [翩々] [E] fluttering

[N] ⓒ Ⓐ ～たる蝶々 a fluttering butterfly.

♦ へんぽん [翩翻]

べんべん [便々] [E] protuberant

[N] ⓒ Ⓐ ～たる腹 Ⓔ a protuberant belly; a potbelly.

へんぽん [翩翻] [E] fluttering

[Av] ⓒ Ⓐ 旗が～と風に翻った the flag fluttered in the wind.

♦ へんぺん [翩々]

[N] ～になる become blind drunk; drink oneself into a stupor; ⓥ ⓢ get pissed.

♦ ぐでんぐでん ♦ へべれけ ♦ ほろり

ほ

ほいほい recklessly; indulgently

[Av] ⓒ ～(と)引き受ける readily take *sth* on; accept *sth* without much thought. ⓒ いつも～(と)付き合ってくる be ready to meet (*sb*) anytime. [する] ⓢ 子供に～する pamper a child; indulge a child.

ぼうだ [滂沱] [E] copious

[Av] ⓒ ～と涙を流す ⓢ shed copious tears; ⓘ cry a river.

ぼーっ roar; whoosh; daze; dimly

[Av] ～と火がつく catch fire. ～と霞んでいる be shrouded in mist. ～と見える be vaguely visible. ～と眺める look vacantly (at *sth*). 法螺貝を～と吹く blow a conch horn.
[Aj] ～としている be absent-minded; be in a daze.
[N] ～となる be dazed; be numbed.

♦ ぼんやり

ぼうばく [茫漠] [E] vague; vast

[N] ⓒ Ⓐ ～たる ❶ vague; obscure. ❷ vast limitless; boundless.

♦ もうろう [朦朧]

ぼーぼー toot; roar; blaze

[Av] 灯台が～と霧笛を鳴らした the

light house blew its foghorn. 火は〜と燃えていた the fire was blazing.

ほーん bong; boing; boom
[Av] ⓐ 炎が〜と上がる the fire burst into flame. ⓐ 〜と壁にぶつかる hit the wall with a resounding bang.

ほかほか warm; steamy; rashly
[Av] ⓐ 〜と事をする ❶ do *sb* forcefully. ❷ act on impulse.
[Aj] 〜(と)した布団 a warm bed.
[N] 〜の饅頭 a steaming hot bean-jam bun. 〜になる warm up.
[する] 背中が〜する feel/be warm.

ぽかぽか warm; repeatedly
[Av] 頭を〜(と)殴られる hit *sb* repeatedly in the face; pummel *sb*.
[Aj] 〜(と)した日 a warm day.
[N] 縁側は〜だ it is warm and comfortable on the balcony.

ぽかり blankly; open-mouthed
[Av] 口を〜と開ける open one's mouth (in amazement). ⓐ 頭を〜と殴られる hit *sb* hard in the face. ⓐ 〜とやられる be hit hard (in the face). 船は凪いだ海に〜と浮かんでいた the ship drifted on the becalmed sea.
♦ ぶかり

ぽかん blankly; open-mouthed
[Av] 〜口をと突っ立てぃいる just stand there in a daze; stand there absentmindedly. 〜と口を開ける open one's mouth (in amazement). 〜と時間に穴が開く be suddenly left with spare time on one's hands. ⓐ 一発〜とやる give *sb* a whack (over the head). 西瓜が〜と割れた the watermelon split open.
[Aj] 〜としている be absent-minded; be in a daze. 〜とした顔つき a bewildered expression; a vacant look.
♦ うっとり ♦ ぼーっ

ぽきっ snap; snapping
[Av] 木の枝が〜と折れた the branch snapped in two. 骨が〜と折れた the bone snapped.
♦ ふっつり ♦ ぽっくり

ぽきぽき snapping; cracking
[Av] 〜(と)小枝を折る snapp off a twig. 〜(と)指を鳴らす make one's knuckles crack.
♦ めりめり

ほくほく flaky; fluffy; content
[Av] 〜(と)喜ぶ be delighted (with oneself). ⓐ 〜(と)歩く saunter; amble. ⓐ 〜(と)頷く nod one's head; bob one's head up and down.

ホクホク

[Aj] 彼は〜とした顔で結果を発表した he presented his findings with a beaming face. 〜(と)した食感 (have) a fluffy bite; (have) a flaky texture.
[N] 彼は成功して〜だ he is chuffed with his success; he can't conceal his glee over his success.
[する] 〜する beam; be all smiles.

ぼけっ idly; vacantly

[する] ⓒ〜とする be idle; lie around; ⓒ loaf one's time away.
♦ ぶらぶら ♦ ぶらり

ぼこっ gaping; wide-open

[する] 柵に〜と穴が空いていた there was a gaping hole in the fence.
♦ くわっ ♦ ぱくり

ぼこぼこ hollow; dented; burble

[Av] 鍋が〜(と)凹んでいる the pan is (heavily) dented. 〜(と)音がする make a hollow sound; sound hollow. 温泉が〜(と)湧き出る the onsen burbles. ⓢ〜にする hit sb hard (in the face).
♦ ぺこぺこ

ぼそっ vacantly; idly; lazily

[する] 〜と呟く mutter sth absent-mindedly. ⓢ〜と立っている stand around idly.

ポタポタ

[Aj] ⓢ〜とした顔つきで窓の外を眺める stare out of the window with a blank expression on one's face.
♦ あっけらかん

ぼそぼそ subdued; flavorless

[Av] 〜(と)話す talk in a subdued voice; talk under one's breath. ⓐ〜(と)生きる live a colorless life.
[Aj] 〜(と)したパン stale bread.
[N] 〜になったパン bread that has gone stale.
♦ ごにょごにょ ♦ ぶすぶす

ほそぼそ [細々] thinly; barely

[Av] 〜と暮らす eke out a living.
[Aj] 〜(と)した声 a frail voice. 〜(と)した腕 slender wrists.
♦ こまごま [細々]

ぼたっ blobbing; splatting

[Av] バターを〜と床に落とす let a blob of butter fall on the floor.

ぼたぼた dripping; thick

[Av] 液が〜(と)滴った the fluid dripped down in thick drops.
[Aj] ⓒ〜(と)した泥 thick mud.

ぽたぽた dripping; trickling

[Av] 〜(と)天井から雨漏りがした water leaked from the ceiling drop by drop. 彼が〜(と)涙を流し始めた

he began to shed tears one by one.
♦ たらたら ♦ ぽとぽと ♦ ぽろぽろ

ぼちぼち slowly; leisurely

[A] 〜(と)始めようか shall we slowly begin? 植物園を〜(と)散歩する have a leisurely walk around the botanical gardens. 斑が〜(と)首にある have speckles scattered around one neck. 水滴が〜(と)落ちている (thick) drops are falling steadily.
♦ ばらばら

ぽちぽち splotching; splattering

[A] ワインが〜(と)入荷している the wine comes in in fits and starts. 雨垂れが〜(と)落ちている (thick) raindrops are falling steadily. 暗証番号を〜(と)押す punch in one's PIN.
♦ ぴちぴち

ぽちゃぽちゃ splashing; chubby

[A] 〜(と)水遊びをする splash around in the water. 〜(と)太った赤ちゃん a chubby little baby.
♦ ちゃぽちゃぽ ♦ ばちゃばちゃ

ほっ sigh; breath

[A] 〜と胸を撫で下ろす hold one's chest with relief. 〜と息を吐く take a deep breath.
[する] 〜とする be relieved; heave a sigh of relief.

ぽっ slightly; suddenly

[A] 〜と顔を赤らめる blush (at the sight of sb). 火が〜と燃え上がった the flame (suddenly) flared up. 〜と道路に飛び出す dash out into the street. ⓐ 〜と育った be raised in idleness.

ぽっかり warmly; dimly; suddenly

[A] ⓐ 〜(と)目が覚めた be aroused from one's slumber. 花が〜(と)咲いた the flowers burst into bloom.
[A] 〜とした懐炉 a comforting pocket warmer.

ぽっくり snapping; swelling

[A] 〜(と)行く pass away suddenly. ⓒ 〜(と)死ぬ drop dead. 息が〜(と)絶えた his breathing suddenly ceased. 枝が〜(と)折れた the branch snapped. ⓐ 〜(と)膨らむ softly swell up. 馬が〜(と)歩いた the horse trotted along clipperdy-clop.
♦ ふっつり ♦ ぽっくり ♦ ぽきっ

ほっそり slim; slender; delicate

[A] 〜(と)見える色 a color that makes you look slim. 〜(と)した娘 a slender girl.
♦ すらっ ♦ すらり ♦ すんなり

ぽっちゃり plump; chubby

[A] 〜(と)した女の子 a chubby little

girl. 〜(と)したほっぺ chubby cheeks. 〜(と)した頬 chubby cheeks.

♦ ぶくぶく ♦ むっつり

ぽってり plump; thick; full

[Aj] 〜(と)した少年 a fat-looking youth. 〜(と)した唇 thick lips.

ぽっちり slightly; a little; just

[Av] ⓒ お金は〜しかない I have only a bit of money left. ⓒ ほんの〜しか食べない eat only a few morsels. 梅の蕾が〜(と)膨らんでいる only one apricot bud was beginning to swell. Ⓐ 眠い目を〜(と)開く wake up with one's eyes wide open.

♦ ちょっぴり

ぽつぽつ bit by bit; scattered

[Av] ⓒ もう〜(と)始めよう let's begin. ⓒ 〜(と)進める proceed bit by bit; make steady progress. 雨が〜(と)降り始めた it started to rain in stops and starts; there was a scattering of rain. 人が〜(と)集まってきた people began to gather one by one. [N] 彼かの顔に〜が出来た he had pimples in his face.

♦ しずしず ♦ そろそろ

ぽつぽつ [勃々] [E] spirited

[Aj] ⓒⓐ 〜としている be in high spirits; be animated; be full of zest.

[N] ⓒⓐ 〜たる spirited; animated; energetic.

ぽつぽつ dotted; scattered

[Av] 家が〜(と)散らばっている houses are scattered (throughout the area). 注文が〜(と)入っている orders are coming in fits and starts. 話を〜(と)語る tell a story bit by bit.

ぽつり isolated; intermittently

[Av] が〜と蛙の顔に当たった a raindrop fell right on the frog's nose. ベルトが〜と切れた the belt suddenly snapped in two. 〜と呟く mutter sth. 背広に〜と穴が空いている there is a (small) hole in my business suit. 〜と一人座る sit all by oneself.

ぽつん isolated; intermittently

[Av] 雨垂れが〜と顔に当たった a (thick) raindrop fell right on my face. 〜と呟く mutter sth. 〜と立っている stand all by oneself.

ぼてぼて heavy; bulky; big

[Av] ⓒ 彼が〜(と)太っている he is really fat. ⓒ 〜に着ぶくれる cover oneself in thick (layers of) clothing. [Aj] 〜(と)した切れ地 thick, heavy cloth.

ポトポト   ボンヤリ

ぽとぽと dripping; trickling
- 雨が～(と)軒先から落ちた water steadily dripped from the eaves.
- ◆たらたら ◆ぽたぽた ◆ぽろぽろ

ぼやぼや careless; disheveled
- Ⓐ ～と燃える burn briskly.
- Ⓐ ～した髪 disheveled hair.
- ～する be careless; fail to pay attention, be inattentive. ～するな watch out! look out!
- ◆うかうか ◆うっかり

ぽりぽり crunching; scratching
- 煎餅を～(と)噛む munch one a rice cracker. 頭を～(と)かく scratch one's head.
- ◆かりかり ◆こりこり

ほろほろ dropping; crumbling
- 涙が～(と)落ちた tears ran down her cheeks. 花びらが～(と)落ちた the petals fell (to the ground). 口の中で～(と)崩れる fall apart in one's mouth. ～(と)鳴く山鳥 a gurgling mountain bird. Ⓐ 敵を～(と)散らす disperse the enemy.

ぽろぽろ dripping; trickling
- 涙が～(と)頬を伝わって溢れた thick tears rolled down her cheeks.
- ◆たらたら ◆ぽたぽた ◆ぽろぽろ

ほろり tipsy; moved; touched
- ～と酔う be tipsy; be slightly intoxicated. 葉が～と落ちる the leaves are softly falling.
- Ⓝ ～となる become tipsy; become slightly intoxicated.
- ～とする be touched; be moved. ～とさせる話 a moving story; a touching story.

ほんのり slightly; faintly
- ～(と)頬を染める get flustered; grow red in the face.
- ～(と)した梅の香り the faint fragrance of plum-blossom. ～(と)した甘み faintly sweet. ～(と)怖い話 a creepy story.
- ◆うっすら

ぽんぽん popping; snappishly
- 花火が～(と)打ち上げられた fireworks were set off. 鼓を～(と)鳴らす tap on a *tsuzumi*. Ⓒチケットが～(と)売れた Ⓒ① the (concert) tickets were selling like hotcakes. 文句が～(と)出てきた the complaints were coming thick and fast.
- Ⓝ お腹が～になる be full; have eaten one's fill; Ⓒ① be stuffed.

ぼんやり faintly; vacantly; idly
- ～(と)見える be vaguely visible. ～(と)日を送る spend one's days in

idleness. 〜(と)口を開ける open one's mouth in astonishment. 〜(と)海を眺める gaze vacantly at the sea. Ⓐ 〜(と)した男 a dim-witted fellow; a dunce. 記憶が〜(と)している have no clear recollection.

♦ ぼーっ

ほんわか warm; snug; cozy

Ⓐ 〜(と)したムード a comfortable/cozy mood.

ま

まごまご confused; flustered

する 〜する be at a loss (what to do).

♦ うろうろ ♦ おたおた

まざまざ plainly; vividly

Ⓐ その光景が〜(と)私の記憶に残っている the scene remains in my memory vividly. 実力の不足を〜(と)思い知られる become fully aware of one's limitations.

♦ ありあり ♦ くっきり ♦ はっきり

まじまじ staring; fixedly

Ⓐ 〜(と)相手の顔を見つめる gaze steadily at sb; stare one's opponent hard in the face. Ⓐ 〜(と)嘘をつく tell lies without batting an eye.
する Ⓐ 〜(と)する hesitate; waver.

flinch. Ⓐ 目は〜する blink one's eyes; be wide awake.

♦ じろじろ ♦ じろり ♦ まんじり

まったり rich; laid-back

Ⓐ 〜(と)した味 a rich/full-bodied taste. 〜(と)した時間 relaxing time; time to relax. 〜(と)した人 a laid-back person.

まんじり napping; staring

Ⓐ ⓐ 人を〜(と)見つめる stare at *sb*.
する ⓐ 〜ともしない do not sleep a wink; be wide awake.

♦ じろじろ ♦ じろり ♦ まじまじ

まんまん [満々] Ⓔ brimming

Ⓝ ⓔ 自信〜だ be full of self-confidence.

まんまん [漫々] Ⓔ vast; limitless

Ⓝ ⓒⓐ 〜たる vast limitless; boundless.

♦ かいかい [怪々] ♦ ばくばく [漠々]

み

みしみし creaking; groaning

Ⓐ 床が〜(と)いう the floor creaks. 屋根が雪の重みで〜(と)音を立てる the roof groans under the weight of the snow. Ⓐ 弟子を〜(と)遣っ付ける

train an apprentice hard; work an apprentice in hard.

する ～する creak; groan.

♦ がたぴし ♦ きしきし ♦ ぎちぎち

みっちり strictly; hard; fully

Av 芸を～(と)教え込む train/drill sb hard in an art. ～(と)腕を磨く practice sth hard; apply oneself to sth.

♦ びしびし

みゃくみゃく [脈々] E continuous

N ～たる continuous; unbroken; uninterrupted.

♦ めんめん [綿々]

む

むかっ sick; nauseating; angry

Av ～とくる feel sick (to one's stomach); be disgusted; be stomach-turning. 腐臭に～とくる get nauseous from a rotten smell.

する ～とする ge fly into a (sudden) rage; hit the ceiling; blow one's top; go ballistic; be pissed off.

むかむか angry; offended; sick

する ～する ❶ fly into a (sudden) rage; hit the ceiling; blow one's top; go ballistic; be pissed off. ❷ feel sick (to one's stomach); be disgusted; be stomach-turning.

むくむく rising; plump; shaggy

Av 煙が～(と)家から湧き出た smoke billowed forth from the house. 国家主義が～(と)頭をもたげてきた nationalism reared its (ugly) head. ～(と)起き上がる veer up; rise. ～と蠢く筋肉 a writhing mass of muscles. ～(と)吃る stammer sth with a quivering mouth.

Av ～した赤ちゃん a chubby baby. ～した毛 a shaggy coat (of hair).

むざむざ helplessly; easily

Av ～(と)諦める give up without making an effort. ～(と)手放す part with sth without regret. ～(と)引っかかる be easily taken in; be easily duped. ～(と)折角のチャンスを見逃す miss a chance in a lifetime; let a golden opportunity slip.

むしむし hot; humid; sultry

する ～する be sultry; be muggy.

♦ むんむん

むしゃくしゃ depressed; vexed

する ～する ❶ feel depressed; be down in the dumps. ❷ be vexed; be on edge; be in a foul mood.

♦ いらいら ♦ くさくさ ♦ じりじり

むしゃむしゃ munch; unkempt

[Av] ⓢ 髪を〜(と)生やす let one's hair grow rampant. 〜(と)食べる eat without manners; munch one's food.

むずむず eager; impatient; itchy

[Av] ⓢ 〜言う mutter; grumble. 虫歯が〜(と)夜通し痛んだ the bad tooth ached all night.
[Aj] 〜(と)した不快感 an uncomfortable sense of foreboding.
[する] 背中が〜する have an itching back. 腕が〜する be eager to do *sth*; can't wait to do *sth*; ⓘ champ at the bit. 口を出したくて〜する be dying to say *sth*.

♦ うずうず ♦ ぶつぶつ

むっくり abruptly; slowly; plump

[Av] 〜(と)起き上がる get up heavily; rise slowly. 〜(と)太っている be fat; be plump.
[Aj] 〜(と)した子 a plump child. ⓐ 〜(と)した ❶ wholesome. ❷ refined.

むっちり plump; chubby; sullen

[Av] ⓐ 〜(と)黙りこくる maintain sullen silence.
[Aj] 〜(と)している ❶ be chubby; be plump. ❶ be sullen; be taciturn. 〜(と)した足 chubby legs. ⓐ 〜(と)した返事 a sullen answer.

♦ ぶくぶく ♦ ぽっちゃり ♦ ぶすり

むっつり plump; chubby; sullen

[Av] 〜(と)押し黙る maintain a sullen silence. 〜(と)黙り込む fall into a sullen silence.
[Aj] 〜(と)した態度 a sullen attitude. 〜(と)した男 a taciturn man. 〜(と)している ❶ be chubby; be plump. ❶ be sullen; be taciturn.

♦ ぶくぶく ♦ ぽっちゃり ♦ ぶすり

むにゃむにゃ mumbling; murmuring

[Av] 〜(と)言う mumble; mutter. 〜(と)言葉を濁す mumble a vague answer. 〜(と)寝言を言う mumble in one's sleep.

♦ もぐもぐ

むらむら [群々] irresistibly; horny

[Av] 怒りが〜(と)湧く feel (the) anger surge up (inside oneself). 〜(と)沸く欲望 an irresistible desire. 〜(と)起こる好奇心 an irresistible curiosity. 〜(と)湧いてくる well up. ⓐ 〜(と)暮らす live together. 〜(と)寄せていく throng to (a place).
[する] ⓥ ⓢ 〜する ⓢ feel horny; be turned on.

むんむん stuffy; sultry; steamy

[Aj] 〜(と)した暑さ oppressive heat. 〜(と)した残暑 lingering sultry summer heat. 〜(と)した雰囲気 an oppressive/sultry atmosphere.

[S] 〜する be stuffy; be sultry; be streamy; be oppressive.

♦ むしむし

め

めいめい [明々] [E] brightly lit; lit up
[Av] © ネオンが〜と灯る the neon lights shone brightly.
[Aj] © 〜とした都会の灯 the city's bright lights.

♦ あかあか

めきめき markedly; rapidly
[Av] 〜(と)進歩する make remarkable/rapid progress. 〜(と)上達する improve markedly. 俳優として〜(と)売り出す become popular as an actor/actress. 小説で〜(と)売り出す gain publicity through a novel.

めそめそ sobbing; weeping
[Av] 〜(と)泣く sob/weep/whimper.
[Aj] 〜(と)した奴 a whiner.
[S] 〜する sob/weep. 〜するな stop whining! cheer up!

♦ さめざめ ♦ しくしく

めためた pulp; messed-up
[Av] 〜に殴られる be beaten to pulp; be beaten up hard. 〜に負ける suffer a crushing defeat; be destroyed.

[N] 体が〜だ my body is broken.

めちゃくちゃ absurd; extreme
[Av] 〜怒られる be extremely angry. 〜楽しい be extremely enjoyable.
[N] 〜な話 a confused story. 〜な値段 a ridiculous price. 〜だ be a mess; be preposterous; be a disaster. 〜になる become disorderly; become messed-up.

めちゃめちゃ disorderly; absurd
[Av] 〜に壊れる be smashed into smithereens.
[N] 〜だ be confused; be messed-up.

めっきり remarkably; noticeably
[Av] 〜(と)老け込む age a lot; grow old fast. 〜(と)来ない show up seldomly. 〜(と)寒くなる become noticeably colder. 〜(と)涼しい be noticeably cooler.

めらめら flare up; ignite; nimbly
[Av] 火が〜(と)燃え移った the flames spread quickly. ⓐ 〜(と)抜け出る steal out effortlessly.
[Aj] © 〜(と)した希望 a burning desire.

♦ へらへら

めりめり splintering; cracking
[Av] 木が〜(と)倒れた the tree fell

over with a splintering crack. 垣が〜(と)いった the fence creaked.
- ♦ ぽきぽき

めろめろ drunk; infatuated

[N] 〜だ be madly in love; ⓘ be head over heels. 〜になる become blind drunk; drink oneself into a stupor; Ⓥ Ⓢ get pissed. Ⓐ 〜(と)剥げる peel off easily. Ⓐ 〜(と)泣く cry easily; ⓘ be a cry-baby.
- ♦ ぐでんぐでん ♦ へべれけ ♦ べろべろ

めんめん [綿々] E continuous

[N] Ⓒ 〜たる continuous; unbroken; uninterrupted.
- ♦ みゃくみゃく [脈々]

も

もうもう [濛々] E dense; thick

[N] Ⓒ 〜たる霞 dense fog; thick fog.

もうろう [朦朧] E dim; vague

[Av] Ⓒ 〜と見える be vaguely visible.
[Aj] Ⓒ 〜としている feel faint; feel groggy; Ⓒ be dopey.
[N] Ⓒ 〜たる dim; vague; indistinct.
- ♦ ぼうばく [茫漠]

もくもく rising; billowing

[Av] 煙が〜(と)空へ立ち上った the smoke billowed up to the sky. 彼が〜(と)筋肉を強直させた he flexed his muscles. 湯が〜(と)湧き出した the hot water welled up.

もくもく [黙々] E silent; mute

[Av] Ⓒ 〜と働く work silently; work in silence.
[Aj] Ⓒ 〜としている remain silent; be mute.

もぐもぐ chewing; mumbling

[Av] 〜食べる munch (one's food). 牛が〜(と)草を食う the cow chews (the) grass. Ⓒ 〜(と)口ごもる mumble; falter. Ⓐ 袂の中を〜(と)探る search (the pocket in) one's sleeve for *sth*.
- ♦ むにゃむにゃ

もこもこ fluffy; lumpy

[Av] 雲が〜(と)湧き出した clouds billowed (in the distance). 〜(と)盛り上がる筋肉 bulging muscles.
[Aj] 〜(と)した猫 a fluffy cat.

もさっ vacantly; dully

[Av] 〜とつっ立っている stand around vacantly/absentmindedly.
[Aj] 〜とした be unattractive; be unsophisticated; be unrefined. 〜としている be absentminded; be distracted.

もさもさ hairy; dense; dull
- [A] 雑草が〜(と)蔓延る the weeds grow dense/rampant. 〜(と)食べる eat sluggishly.
- [する] ⓒ 〜するな pay attention! ⓒ look sharp!

もしゃもしゃ scraggly; unkempt
- [A] ⓒ 〜した髪の毛 unruly hair. ⓐ 〜した心持ち a bellicose mood.

もじゃもじゃ tousled; unkempt
- [A] 〜(と)した髭 an unruly beard. 〜(と)した犬 a shaggy dog.
- [N] 〜の髪 tousled hair.
- ◆ ばさばさ ◆ ばさり ◆ はたはた

もじもじ fidgeting; wriggling
- [する] 〜する hesitate; fidget; ; be restless; be bashful. 椅子の上で〜(と)する shift about in one's chair.
- ◆ たじたじ

もそもそ creeping; squirming
- [A] 虫が〜(と)這い回った the insect wriggled around. 〜(と)動き回る move about restlessly. 〜(と)立ち上がる get up restlessly.
- ◆ にゅるにゅる

もたもた slowly; tardily
- [A] 〜(と)走る run slowly. 〜(と)歩く dawdle; walk tardily.
- [する] 〜する be slow; dawdle; lag behind.
- ◆ ぐずぐず ◆ のそのそ ◆ のろのろ

もちもち chewy; doughy
- [A] 〜(と)したうどん doughy *udon*. 〜(と)した食感 a chewy texture. 〜(と)した肢体 plump limbs. 〜(と)した肌 puffy skin.
- ◆ しこしこ

もっさり tasteless; dim-witted
- [A] 〜とつっ立っている stand around goofily.
- [A] 〜(と)した男 an unrefined man; a clumsy man. 〜(と)した髪の毛 dense hair.

もっちり springy; puffy
- [A] 〜(と)した食感 a chewy/springy consistency.

もやもや hazy; misty; foggy
- [A] 煙で〜(と)した部屋 a smoke-filled room; a room clogged with smoke. 〜(と)した記憶 a vague recollection.
- [N] 胸の〜を晴らす lift one's gloom. 胸の〜を吹き飛ばす give vent to one's resentment/discontent.
- [する] 頭が〜(と)する ⓒ feel fuzzy; ⓒ feel foggy.

もわっ full; suffocating

- Av ⓒ〜と広がる髪 lush hair.
- AJ 〜とした熱気 suffocating heat. 〜とした匂い an overwhelming stench; a nauseating stench. 〜とした煙 asphyxiating smoke.
- する 〜とする湿気 suffocating humidity. 〜とする匂い an overwhelming stench; a nauseating stench.

♦ つんつん ♦ ぷんぷん

もんもん [悶々] E discontent

- N ⓒⒶ 〜たる老人 a discontented old man/woman.

や

やいやい pressingly; demandingly

- Av ⓒ 〜言う urge sb; press sb. ⓒ 〜と貰いたがる want sth really badly. ⓒ 〜と小遣いをせがまれる pester (one's parents) for pocket money.

♦ がみがみ

やきもき fretting; worried

- AJ 〜(と)気をもむ frett over sth.
- する 〜する frett; worry; be anxious.

やんわり softly; gently; mildly

- Av 〜(と)子供を叱る scold a child mildly. 〜(と)断る refuse sth gently. 〜(と)握る hold sth gently.

AJ 〜(と)した肌触り feel soft to the skin. 〜(と)した口調で in a mild tone. 〜(と)した言い方 a gently way of saying sth; a soft expression. 〜(と)した春の日差し the soft rays of spring.

♦ うらうら

ゆ

ゆうゆう [悠々] quietly; easily

- Av 〜と勝つ win easily; win hands-down. 〜と暮らす live an easy life; live in comfort.
- N ⓒⒶ 〜たる ❶ quiet; calm. ❷ leisurely; slow; deliberate. ❸ endless; vast; boundless.

ゆうよう [悠揚] E self-possessed

- N ⓒⒶ 〜たる self-possessed; free and easy; calm; composed.

ようよう [洋々] E wide; broad

- N ⓒⒶ 〜たる川 the wide river. ⓔ 前途〜たる (have) a bright future (ahead of one).

ゆうよう [揚々] E triumphant

- AJ 〜としている be in high spirits; be elated; ⓘ with colors flying.
- N ⓔ 〜たる triumphant; elated; exultant.

ゆさゆさ swaying; shaking
[Av] 太（ふと）い枝（えだ）が風（かぜ）で〜（と）揺（ゆ）れた the big branches swayed in the wind. 家（いえ）が地震（じしん）で〜（と）揺（ゆ）れた the house rocked due to the earthquake.

♦ ゆらゆら

ゆっくり slowly; leisurely
[Av] 〜（と）腰（こし）をあげる rise slowly; stand up slowly. 〜（と）話（はなし）す talk at ease. 〜（と）歩（ある）く walk leisurely.
[する] 〜する unwind; take some rest.

♦ のたのた ♦ のらのら

ゆったり calm; comfortable
[Av] 気（き）を〜持（も）て relax! loosen up! 〜（と）寛（くつろ）ぐ get comfortable; ⓘ wind down.
[Aj] 〜（と）したセーター a comfortable sweater.

ゆらゆら swaying; rocking
[Av] ランプが〜（と）揺（ゆ）れた the lamp (gently) swayed back and forth. 枝（えだ）が風（かぜ）で〜（と）揺（ゆ）れた the branches swayed in the wind. 水（みず）に映（うつ）った日差（ひざ）しが〜（と）揺（ゆ）れた the sun rays danced on the water.

♦ ゆさゆさ

ゆらりゆらり swaying; rocking
[Av] 船（ふね）が〜（と）波間（はま）に揺（ゆ）られた the boat swayed gently on the waves; the waves gently rocked the boat.

ゆるゆる [緩々] loosely; leisurely
[Av] ⓐ 〜（と）茶（ちゃ）をすする drink one's tea leisurely. ⓒ 〜（と）進（すす）む proceed slowly. ⓒ 〜（と）話（はなし）す talk at ease.
[N] 〜のズボン baggy trousers.

♦ ざっくり

よ

よくよく [翼々] ⒺⒺ prudent
[Aj] ⒺⓐⓐⒶⓐ 小心（しょうしん）〜とした男（おとこ） a timid man; a cowardly man.

よたよた waddling; tottering
[Av] 〜（と）歩（ある）く waddle; totter; stagger.
[Aj] 〜した足取（あしど）り Ⓒⓘⓘ be on penguin legs.
[N] 〜になる become unsteady (on one's legs).
[する] 〜する waddle; totter; stagger.

♦ よろよろ

よちよち toddling; tottering
[Av] 赤（あか）ん坊（ぼう）が〜（と）歩（ある）き出（だ）した the baby waddled along.
[する] 〜する toddle; totter; stagger.

よぼよぼ doddering; tottering
[Av] 〜（と）歩（ある）く老人（ろうじん） a doddering old man. 杖（つえ）に頼（たよ）って〜（と）歩（ある）く totter along leaning on a walking stick.

よれよれ shabby; threadbare

N ～のズボン shabby trousers. ～になる become warn out; become threadbare. ～のスカート a tired-looking skirt.

する ～する be shabby; be threadbare.

よろよろ staggering; faltering

Av ～(と)歩く stagger; falter. ～(と)立ち上がる stagger to one's feet.

する ～する stagger; reel; falter.

♦ よたよた

ら

らいらい [磊々] E rocky; magnanimous

AJ ～Ⓔたる砂礫 heaps of pebbles. ～Ⓔの(と)した人 a large-hearted person; a magnanimous person.

らくらく [楽々] comfortably

する ～と勝つ win easily; win comfortably. ～と試験に通る ① pass an examination with colors flying; ① sail through an examination.

らんまん [爛漫] E glorious

Av ～(と)咲く be in full bloom; Ⓔ bloom in profusion.
N Ⓔ～たる桜花 full-blown cherry blossoms.

らんらん [爛々] E glaring; flaming

する ～Ⓔⓐとする目 glaring eyes.

り

りゅうりゅう [隆々] E prosperous

N Ⓔ～たる ❶ prosperous; thriving. ❷ muscular; brawny sinewy.

りんりん jingling; tinkling

Av ～(と)鳴る鈴 a jingling bel.

りんりん [凛々] E severe; intense

AJ ～Ⓔたる awe-inspiring; awesome. ～Ⓔたる寒気 severe cold.

る

るいるい [塁々] E heaps; countless

N Ⓔ～たる in heaps; in profusion.

るんるん euphoric; buoyant

Av ～(と)弾む心 a buoyed-up heart.
AJ ～(と)した気分 a euphoric mood.

れ

れいれい [麗々] E ostentatious

N Ⓔ～たる ostentatious; pretentious; showy; gaudy.

れきれき [歴々] ⓔ obvious; clear

Ⓝ ⓔ 〜たる plain; clear; obvious.

れろれろ jabber; splutter

Ⓐᵥ ⓢ 〜言う jabber. ⓢ 〜(と)呟く mutter *sth* incomprehensibly.

Ⓝ ⓢ 酔っ払って口が〜だ be unable to talk straight. ⓢ 言葉が〜になる become slurred in one's speech.

♦ **ろれろれ**

ろ

ろうろう [朗々] ⓔ sonorous

Ⓐᵥ ⓔ 〜と響く声 a rich/resonant voice.

Ⓝ ⓔ 〜たる clear; sonorous; clarion.

ろくろく [碌々] ⓔ idly; hardly

Ⓐᵥ ⓔ 〜勉強もしない do not study anywhere near enough; hardly study. ⓔ 〜眠れなかった haven't slept anywhere near enough.

Ⓐⱼ ⓔⓐ 〜としている be idle; spend one's time in idleness.

ろれろれ Ⓐ slurring; stuttering

Ⓐᵥ ⓐ 〜言う slur. ⓐ 〜(と)舌が回らない be unable to articulate one's words.

Ⓝ ⓐ 酔っ払って口が〜だ be unable to talk straight. ⓐ 言葉が〜になる become slurred in one's speech.

♦ **ろれろれ**

わ

わーわー boohoo; blubber

Ⓐᵥ 赤ん坊が〜(と)泣いている the baby is screaming.

わいわい clamor; uproar

Ⓐᵥ 〜騒ぎ立てる raise an uproar; ⓒ raise a ruckus. 〜言う make a fuss.

す 〜やる make merry.

♦ **がやがや** ♦ **ざわざわ** ♦ **わーわー**

わーわー waah!; crying; jeering

Ⓐᵥ 〜(と)泣く cry loudly. 人の失敗〜(と)囃し立てる jeer at *sb's* mistake; make fun of *sb's* mistake.

♦ **がやがや** ♦ **ざわざわ** ♦ **わーわー**

わくわく excitedly; nervously

す 〜する be exited/anxious.

♦ **いそいそ**

わさわさ restless; lively; busy

Ⓐⱼ 〜した雰囲気 a lively atmosphere. 社内が早朝から〜している the office had been in a state of

ワサワサ

excitement since early morning.
♦ そわそわ

わなわな trembling; shivering

[Av] 怒りに～と震える tremble with rage.

[する] ～する tremble; shiver.

♦ こわごわ ♦ びくびく

Animals, Birds and Insects

ANIMALS

bear	熊 (くま)	グオー	
bee	蜂 (はち)	ブーンブーン	
cat	猫 (ねこ)	ニャーニャー / ニャン	
cow	牛 (うし)	モーモー	
deer	鹿 (しか)	ビッ	
dog	犬 (いぬ)	ワンワン / キャンキャン	
elephant	像 (ぞう)	パオーン	
fox	狐 (きつね)	ケンケン	
frog	蛙 (かえる)	ケロケロ	
goat	山羊 (やぎ)	メーメー	
horse	馬 (うま)	ヒヒーン	
lion	獅子 (しし)	ガオー	
monkey	猿 (さる)	ウキー / ウキウキ / ウキキー	
mouse	鼠 (ねずみ)	チューチュー	
pheasant	雉 (きじ)	ケンケン / コンコン	
pig	豚 (ぶた)	ブーブー / ブヒブヒ	
rooster	鶏 (にわとり)	コケコッコー	
sheep	羊 (ひつじ)	メーメー	
snake	蛇 (へび)	シュー	

BIRDS

bird (general)	鳥 (とり)	ピチュピチュ	
broad-billed roller	仏法僧 (ぶっぽうそう)	グェーゲゲゲ	
bunting	頬白 (ほおじろ)	チョッチーチョッ / チリリ / チュチュ	
bush warbler	鶯 (うぐいす)	ホーホケキョ	
chick	雛 (ひよこ)	ピヨピヨ	
crane	鶴 (つる)	クーカッカッ / クォーンカッカゥ	
crow	鴉 (からす)	カーカ	
cuckoo	郭公 (かっこう)	カッコー	
domestic duck	鶩 (あひる)	グワッグワッ	
duck	鴨 (かも)	ガーガー	

112

Animals, Birds and Insects

goose	鵞鳥	がちょう	ガッガッ
grosbeak	鵤	いかる	キィーコキィー / キョコキィー
kite	鳶	とび	ピーヒョロロ
litle cuckoo	時鳥	ほととぎす	テッペンカケタカ
magpie	鵲		カシャカシャカシャ / カッカッカッカッ
mountain bird	山鳥	やまどり	ホロホロ
owl	梟	ふくろう	ホーホー
Oriental cuckoo	筒鳥	つつどり	ポンポン
pigeon	鳩	はと	ポッポ
plover	千鳥	ちどり	ピュイ / ピュル / ピピ
quail	鶉	うずら	グワー / ゴワー
shrike	鵙	もず	キィーキィー / ギチギチ
(sky)lark	雲雀	ひばり	ピィチブ / チュルル
sparrow	雀	すずめ	チュンチュン
swallow	燕	つばめ	チョチョビチョチョビ
water rail	水鶏	くいな	キョッキョッ / クヒクヒ
white-eye	目白	めじろ	チィチィチュチィーチィーチィー
woodpecker	啄木鳥	きつつき	カカカカカ

INSECTS

bell cricket	鈴虫	すずむし	リーンリーン
bush cricket	鉦叩き	かねたたき	チン
cicada	蝉	せみ	ジージー / ミーンミーン
cricket	蟋蟀	こおろぎ	コロコロ / キリキリ
giant katydid	轡虫	くつわむし	ガチャガチャ
grass cricket	草雲雀	くさひばり	フィリリリリ
long-horned grasshopper	馬追い	うまおい	スイッチョ
male titillator	藪螽蟖	やぶきり	シュルルル
mole cricket	螻蛄	けら	ジー
pine cricket	松虫	まつむし	チンチロリン
(snowy) tree cricket	邯鄲	かんたん	ルルルル

113

Index

bit by bit 57, 99
biting 9, 14, 56
blank 72
blankly 1, 20, 96
blaring 43, 86
blaze 95
blazing 6, 16
bleating 79
blinking 42, 76
blobbing 97
blow 82
blowing 87, 89
blubber 110
bluntly 48, 50, 61
bobbing 84, 87
boiling 25, 89
boing 96
boisterously 29
bone-dry 8
bong 30, 96
bonk 33
boohoo 6, 110
boom 50, 63, 67, 96
boring 4, 6
bouncing 84
boundless 84
brazenly 7, 43, 70-71
breaking 89
breath 98
breathing 87
breeze 54
briefly 37
bright 1
bright red 1
brightly 39, 79
brightly lit 1, 104
brilliant 8
brilliantly 30, 39-40, 79
brimming 101
briskly 9, 12, 19, 21, 43, 48, 61-62, 73-74

A
a bit 59
abruptly 69-70, 84, 86, 103
absurd 104
aching 17
achoo 23
agitatedly 53
aimlessly 72, 90
airily 92
all out 73
all smiles 5
aloof 61
ample 43, 55, 56
angry 91, 102
anguished 38
aooo 3
ardently 6
aroused 4
at a glance 59
at once 66

B
babbling 66
baggy 14, 87
bam 73
bang 10, 33, 50, 55, 63, 67, 73, 76, 79
banging 36, 43
barely 9, 12, 21, 97
barfing 29
barking 28, 30
bawling 7
beaming 68
beating 33, 75
begging 60
big 27, 99
billowing 105

bristly 64
broad 107
browned 36
brushing 45
bubbling 34, 88, 89
bubbly 88
bulging 87, 88
bulky 66, 99
bump 10, 36
bumpiness 62
buoyant 109
buoyantly 3, 84
burble 97
burning 85
burst 15, 86
burst out 65
bursting 79, 82
bushy 88
busily 1
bustle 39, 64
busy 110
buzzing 91
by accident 59

C
cackle 25, 29
cackling 29
calm 108
calmly 7
candid 37
carefree 71, 73
carefully 41, 65
careless 100
carelessly 3-4
casually 84
chatter 19, 58
chattering 10, 68, 93
chatty 57
cheep 85
cheerfully 3, 15
chewing 14, 105

115

chewy 41, 106
chilly 83, 86
chink 60
chirp 57
chirping 35, 58, 60
chitter 19
choking 29
chop 37, 59
chubby 76, 88, 98, 103
chuckle 6, 23, 29
chug-chug 45
chugging 30-31
churning 28
clack 11, 77
clacking 12
clammy 43
clamor 14, 110
clanging 11, 16, 36, 44
clank 10, 11, 13
clanking 10, 11
clap 59
clapper 16
clapping 76, 79
clattering 9, 10-11, 15, 33-34, 76
clean 38, 47
cleanly 47, 49
clear 47, 110
clearly 2, 19, 25, 39, 73, 77
click 10, 11
clicking 9, 12, 75, 81
clinging 11, 92-93
clinking 9, 11
clip-clop 16
clopping 34
closely 82-83
cluck 57
clump 65
clumping 65
clunk 13

clunking 10
coarse 37
coff-coff 34
coiling 28
cold 22, 86
collapsing 92
come down 50
comfortable 108
comfortably 109
compact 57
compactly 60
complacent 69
complaining 61, 89
completely 5, 31-32, 49-50, 54
composure 16
confused 101
confusedly 91
content 96
continuing 51
continuous 102, 105
coo 25
cool 86
copious 36, 95
copiously 64
corpulent 62
cosily 60
cough 34
coughing 29, 34
countless 109
course 38-39, 44
covetously 12
coweringly 7
cozy 101
crack 73
cracking 9, 11, 76, 96, 104
crackling 80
crammed 18
cramped 31
crash 10, 55, 76

crashing 9, 11, 37
crawling with 5
creak 17
creaking 10, 17-18, 20-21, 101
creamy 66
creeping 106
crestfallen 12
crisp 16, 34, 36, 43, 74-75
crispy 78, 79
croak 7
croaking 29
crumbling 100
crumbly 75, 78
crumpled 23
crumpling 24
crunching 34, 37, 78, 100
crunchy 16, 36, 78
crushing 23
crying 7, 110
cunning 57
curling 28
cursory 37
cut down 77
cut up 48
cute 88
cutting 58

D

dabbling 82
dally 44
damp 42
dangling 90
dark 68
dashing 78
daze 95
dazzling 21
dead drunk 26
decisively 50

deep 25
deeply 25, 37, 43, 46, 50, 61
dejected 12, 29, 30, 40, 48
dejectedly 45
deliberately 41
delicate 98
demandingly 107
dense 105-106
densely 36, 82
dented 92, 97
depressed 22, 102
deserted 16
determinedly 61
difficult 16
difficulties 2
dignified 44, 49, 66
diligently 53
dim 105
dim-witted 106
dimly 95, 98
ding 60
direct 37
disappear 67
disappointed 12
discontent 107
disheveled 100
disorderly 9, 104
distinctly 25
dizzy 27
dot 59
dulled 99
doughy 106
down 48
dozing 5, 30, 32, 66-67
drastically 77
drenched 25, 42, 81-82
dried stiff 14
dried-up 15
drifting 91

dripping 23, 55, 97, 100
drizzling 45, 54
droning 20
drooling 56
dropping 100
drowsily 5
drowsy 67
drumming 68
drunk 94, 105
dry 8-9, 75
dull 67-68, 106
dully 105
dumbstruck 19

E

eager 103
eagerly 4
easily 1, 35, 51, 69, 102, 107
easy 43
ecstatic 4, 22
elated 64
eminent 53
empty 16
energetic 86
enthusiastically 73
entirely 30, 31, 32, 38, 39, 49-50, 54
equal 59
erect 86
eternally 6
euphoric 109
evasive 72
evenly 67
exactly 13, 18, 41, 59, 81, 83
excitedly 3, 110
exhausted 12, 25, 93
exhilarated 5
extreme 104

F

faint 86
faintly 4, 100
fall down flat 49-50
faltering 66, 109
fart 87
fast 48, 79
fast asleep 36
fat 62
fawn 57
fawning 92
fearful 35, 80
fed up 6
fickly 91
fidgeting 106
fidgety 31, 53, 54
fiercely 12, 75
firm 34
firmly 9, 13, 20, 25, 28, 41, 80
fixedly 41, 101
flabby 26, 55, 90
flaky 96
flaming 109
flap 74
flapping 75-76
flare up 104
flashing 77
flashy 22
flat 72
flat broke 49
flatly 19, 80
flattened 92, 93
flavorless 97
flexible 26, 42
flicker 60
flickering 59, 85
flippant 94
flipping 94
flirt 3, 44

117

flirting 63
flirty 57
flittering 56
floating 91
flop 65, 74-75
flopping 35, 92-93
floundering 2
fluently 94
fluffily 92
fluffy 87, 89, 91, 96, 105
flump 65
flurried 64
flustered 1, 7, 101
fluttering 75-76, 78, 85, 95
foggy 106
fondly 42
foolishly 94
forcefully 22
forever 6
forthrightly 39
fragrant 87
frank 37, 38
frankly 48, 61
freely 61, 64, 70
frequently 41, 55, 86
fretting 22, 27, 107
frizzle 60
frizzling 44-45
frothing 2
full 55, 99, 107
fully 15, 41, 89, 102
fuming 92
furious 16
furtively 23, 31
fussily 1
fussy 31

G

gabble 7
gaping 28, 74, 97
garish 29
gasping 6, 53, 73-74
gaudy 22, 29, 33
gently 5, 7, 42, 47, 54, 55, 68, 85, 91-92, 107
giddy 27
giggle 23, 25, 29
giggling 29
glance 60
glancing 46
glaring 21, 28, 109
gleaming 62
glimmer 79
glimmering 21, 59
glimpsing 59
glistening 21
glitter 79
glittering 21
gloomily 4, 45
gloomy 2, 23, 43
glorious 8, 109
glossy 61
glugging 64, 66
glumly 88
gnawing 1, 9
goggling 20
gong 30
gooey 67, 71, 93
gracefully 44
gradually 47, 54, 56, 81
grainy 61
granular 38
grating 86
grazing 52
greasy 19, 70
greatly 28
greedily 12
green 1
grinding 18, 21-22, 27
grinning 68-69
gritty 38-39, 44

groaning 5, 101
grumbling 32
grumpily 16
grunting 5, 89
guffawing 29
gulping 14, 22, 26, 30, 31
gummy 68, 71, 93
gurgling 2, 14, 34, 64, 66
gushing 14, 36, 43, 55
guzzling 14, 26

H

hacking 34
haggard 29
hairy 106
hard 6, 10-11, 13, 20, 27, 31-32, 79-80, 86, 102
hard up 79
hard-hitting 23
hardly 110
harmonious 1
harsh 22
hastily 1
haw-hawing 29
haziness 84
hazy 106
heaps 65, 109
heartily 9, 29
heartrending 40, 46
heavily 48-49, 63, 65, 66, 71, 72
heavy 48, 66, 68, 99
hefty 66
hehehe 93
helplessly 94, 102
helter-skelter 48
hesitantly 2-3, 7
hiss 83

hissing — meow

hissing 44–45, 47
hollow 97
honk 60, 87
hopping 30, 85
horny 103
hot 102
hotly 12
howl 3
howling 83
huff 86
huge 62
humid 102
humming 20, 91
hungry 92
hurriedly 1
hushed 60

I

idlingly 72
idly 72–73, 90, 97, 100, 110
ignite 104
impatient 103
impatiently 4
imposingly 63
in a flash 76
in a line 51, 54
in a lump 54
in a row 51
in detail 34
in motion 58
in shape 44
in swarms 3–5
inadvertently 4
incessant 40
indifferent 56
indiscreetly 28
indulgently 95
industriously 53
infatuated 105
insipid 9

insistent 70, 71
intense 16, 109
intently 40, 61
intermittently 99
intoxicated 67, 94
irresistibly 103
irresolutely 3
irritation 3
isolated 99
itchy 103

J

jabber 110
jagged 17
jam-packed 18
jangle 57
jeering 110
jerkingly 8
jerky 17
jingle 57
jingling 44, 57, 60, 109
jumble 32
jumbled 31
jump 82
jump up 69
jumping 79
just 52, 59, 99
jut out 69

K

keenly 43, 61, 80
kissing 58
klunk 14
knackered 93
knobbly 89
knocking 10, 13, 31, 36

L

laboriously 6
laid-back 101
lapping 81, 93

large 66, 77
laughing 77
lazily 72, 97
lazy 63, 70
leisurely 72–73, 94, 98, 108
lengthy 24
level 56
licking 94, 95
lightly 1, 4, 50, 58, 81, 84–85, 87, 91
limitless 84, 101
limp 25, 26, 89
lined up 51
lit up 1, 104
little 99
little by little 57
lively 2, 19, 54, 78, 86, 110
lob 37
loiteringly 5
long 51
long-winded 4
loose 8, 24, 55, 78
loosely 37, 108
loud 29
loudly 9
lucidly 73
lumbering 71–72
lumpy 61, 105
lurching 27

M

magnanimous 109
magnificent 63
make out 3
markedly 104
meandering 5–6, 40
meaningfully 69
melancholily 6
meow 69

119

mess 31
messed-up 104
messy 9, 24, 31, 34, 93
mewing 69
mewling 6
miaow 69
microwave 60
mildly 107
milled 17
minutely 34
misty 106
mix up 32
moaning 89
moist 5, 42
moonstruck 62
moping 22
morose 46, 61
motionlessly 41
moved 100
moving 63
mow down 77
muddle 31
muddy 67
muffled 87
mumbling 34, 87, 89, 103, 105
munch 103
munching 1, 74
murmuring 38, 103
murmuringly 53
mushy 23-24, 91
mute 105
muttering 34, 88

N

nagging 14, 70
napping 101
narrowly 12
nauseating 102
neat 38
neatly 18, 49, 57, 80

negligently 3
neighing 83
nervous 20, 64, 83
nervously 6-7, 20-21, 29, 110
new 79
nicely 41
nimbly 52, 85, 104
nitpicking 61
nodding 32
nodding off 5, 30
noise 39
noisily 14, 65, 66
non-stop 44, 94
nonchalantly 30, 71-72
notched 17
noticeably 28, 104
numbing 40, 46

O

obvious 110
occasionally 6
offended 102
often 41-42, 55, 58
oily 19
on a whim 90
one by one 64
oozing 40, 46
open-mouthed 2, 96
orderly 44
ostentatious 109
outspoken 8, 50
over the top 62
overflowing 56

P

pain 40
pamper 57
pang 55, 79
panicky 1
panting 6, 53, 73, 77

parched 14, 15
passing 63
patiently 40
patter 81
peacefully 51
pealing 16
peeping 79
penniless 49
perfect 77
perfectly 83
perhaps 84
persistent 71
persistently 46
piercing 22, 28, 46
ping 20
pinging 17
pissed 26, 50
plainly 19, 49, 77, 101
plenty 55, 65, 77, 79
pliant 42, 46
plock 10, 33
ploddingly 72
plonk 50
plop 39, 51, 66
plopping 74
plump 89, 91, 98-99, 102-103
plunge 8
plunging 43, 88
plunk 65
pointed 61
poke 59
poof 87
pop 51
popping 100
pounding 16, 74
pouring 36, 65
pouring heavily 39
pouring steadily 39
prattling 34, 93
precisely 18, 43, 50, 59

pressingly 107
pricking 88
prickling 56
profoundly 48
profusely 64
promptly 38, 62
prosperous 109
protuberant 95
proud; 64
prudent 108
puff 86, 88
puff-puff 50
puffed up 87
puffing 53, 77, 87
puffy 106
puking 29
pulp 104
pulpy 23, 24, 26
punctually 18
pungent 61, 92
purring 35

Q

quack 7
quetly 42
quickly 1, 14, 37-38, 48, 52, 58, 66, 76, 84
quietly 7, 40-41, 53, 83, 107

R

rambling 90
rapidly 28, 48, 52, 64, 68, 104
rapping 36
rashly 96
rasp 17
rasping 31
rattling 9, 10-11, 15, 33, 85
readily 51

recklessly 95
reeling 55
refreshed 47-49, 53
regular 57
relentlessly 80
relieved 38
remarkably 104
repeatedly 28, 36, 58, 96
repetitive 26
resolutely 12, 77
restless 20, 54, 110
restlessly 5, 20-21, 58
retching 29
rich 101
richly 33
rigidly 10
ringing 45, 60
rip 82
rip-off 74
ripping 78, 85
rising 102, 105
roar 95
roaring 3, 63
robust 44
rocking 108
rocky 109
rolling 20, 27-28, 35, 72
roly-poly 35
rotund 27, 52
rough 8, 37, 39, 44
roughly 9, 37
round 27
rudely 15
rugged 32
rumble 48
rumbling 22, 30, 35, 67
rummaging 31
rush 65
rushing 36, 63, 65
rustle 39, 74

rustling 8, 31, 38, 44-45, 74

S

sad 40, 48
saggy 55
satisfaction 69
scattered 78, 99
scraggly 106
scraggy 32
scrape 45, 54
scraping 34
scratch 54
scratching 100
scream 19
screaming 79
screech 19
screeching 17
scrubbing 31
scrutinizing 45, 46
scurry 48
scurrying 8
secretly 32, 81
seeping 46
self-possessed 107
seriously 46
severe 109
shabby 109
shaggy 102
shaking 108
shaky 27
shamelessly 7
sharp 2, 64
shave 45, 54
shhh 40
shining 62
shivering 53, 91, 111
shocked 7
shocking 17, 18
shoo 40
showy 22, 76

121

shredded 61
shrewd 13, 57
shriek 19
shrieking 79
shrill 22, 40
shrivel 60
shuddering 53
sick 102
sigh 86, 98
silence 46
silent 60, 105
silently 40, 45, 83
silver 8
simmer 67
simmering 25
sirupy 71
sizzle 60
sizzling 44-45
skillfully 36
skimming 52
skinny 16
skipping 85
slam 63, 67, 76
slamming 11, 81
slapping 75, 81, 92-93
slashing 38
sleek 50
sleep like a log 22
sleep soundly 22
slender 51, 52, 98
slick 61
sliding 52, 69
slightly 4, 58-59, 98-99, 100
slim 51, 98
slimy 70
slip away 67
slippery 61, 70, 72
slithering 45, 69
slobbering 56
sloppily 54

sloppy 24
sloshing 38, 57, 75, 81
slovenly 62-63
slowly 24, 41-42, 45, 46, 47, 54-55, 72-73, 103, 106, 108
sluggish 55
sluggishly 70, 72-73
slump 10
slumping 35
slurp 47, 82
slurping 47, 52, 61
slurring 110
smack 77, 82
smacking 93
small 57
smarting 47, 85
smartly 80
smiling 68-69
smirking 68-69
smolder 67
smoldering 88
smooth 50-52, 70, 72
smoothly 39, 47, 51-52, 61, 67
snap 73, 75, 80, 96
snapping 9, 74-75, 81, 89, 96, 98
snappishly 100
snappy 74
snarling 14
sneakily 31
sneezing 23
snicker 89
sniff 80
sniff-sniff 91
sniffing 28
sniffle 24
snigger 89
sniggle 6
snipping 58

snoring 22
snort 60
snuffle 24
snug 101
snugly 51, 60, 69, 83
soaked 42, 50, 81
soaking 25, 82
sobbing 40, 104
sodden 40
soft 26, 42, 46, 87, 89, 90
softly 5, 53-54, 91, 107
soggy 23
solemnly 46
solid 64
solidly 9, 13
solitude 29
sonorous 110
soon 54
soothing 51
sopping 23
soppy 24
sordid 67
sorrowful 38
sound 25, 64, 77
spacious 8
sparkle 79
sparkling 21
sparse 78
sparsely 59
speechless 7, 19
spellbound 4
spineless 26
spinning 28
spirited 79, 99
spit 83
spitting 89
splash 39, 66
splashing 43-44, 57, 75-76, 81-82, 98
splattering 82, 98

splatting | tipsy

splatting 97
splintering 104
split 73
splotching 98
splutter 110
spoil 57
spongy 91
sporadically 59
spot on 77
spring up 69
springy 41, 106
sputtering 88
squalid 34
squashed 92-93
squashing 23
squeaking 17-19, 58
squeal 19
squelching 14
squirming 106
squishing 23
staggering 85, 109
stamping 63, 92
starchy 35, 67
staring 20, 45-46, 101
startled 17, 20, 82
startling 17-18
steadily 28, 32, 41, 52, 56, 62
stealthily 32, 53
steamy 96, 103
step 65
stick out 69
sticking 93
sticky 19, 68, 70-71, 92-93
stiff 17-18, 35, 78
stifled 25
stilted 17
stinging 56, 85
stocky 52
stolidly 72

stomping 64
stout 52, 62
straight 43, 47-48, 57, 60
strained 18
strapping 66
strictly 102
strong 33
struggle 41
stubbornly 80
stuffy 103
stuttering 110
stylish 78
subdued 32, 97
substantial 56
successfully 5
successively 51, 53, 64
suck 47
suddenly 8, 12, 14-15, 17, 20, 22, 25, 35, 37, 63, 69, 70, 75-76, 81, 84, 86, 88-89, 98
sufficiently 79
suffocating 107
suggestively 69
sullen 46, 103
sultry 102-103
supple 46, 52
surge 65
surprised 76, 82
swarming 54
swaying 27, 90, 108
swelling 72, 87, 98
swiftly 48, 52, 85
swishing 8, 37, 44, 83, 84
swoop 8
swoosh 8, 43, 74
swooshing 36, 37
syrupy 66

T

tapping 32, 36, 75
tardily 24, 106
tasteless 106
taut 86
tear 73, 82
tearing 78, 85, 94
teary-eyed 5
tedious 3-4, 6, 24, 26
tender 91
tense 32, 86
tensely 21
the end 64
thick 62, 67, 97, 99, 105
thickly 33, 36
thin 18, 94
thinly 4, 39, 97
thorny 2, 64
thorough 29, 64
thoroughly 50, 64-65
thrashing 33
threadbare 109
throbbing 46-47, 64, 86
thrusting 88
thuck 22-23
thud 16, 33, 36, 50, 63, 65, 75-76
thump 14, 16, 33, 36, 65
thumping 55, 64, 74
ticking 10, 31
tickling 32
tidily 18
tidy 80
tightly 13, 18-21, 41, 51, 81-83
timidly 2, 6
tingling 46, 56
tinkle 57
tinkling 109
tipsy 100

123

tiresome 24
titter 89
to the brim 68
tock 33
toddling 64, 108
toot 87, 95
tooting 87
torn 48, 61
totally 49-50, 66
tottering 66, 85, 108
touched 100
tough 13
tousled 106
trailing 52, 54
tramping 65
trampling 76
trembling 35, 80, 91, 111
trickle 60
trickling 55, 59, 97, 100
triumphant 107
trotting 64
trouble 2
trudging 66
trudgingly 62
tsak 22-23
tufty 88
tugging 22
tweet 85
twinkling 56
twisted 26
twisting 26
twitching 79-80
twittering 60
typing 74
tzing 20
tzinging 17

U

uh-huh 91
unevenness 62

unhindered 47, 52
unintentionally 60, 84
unkempt 74, 103, 106
unsteady 84, 90
unyielding 11
uproar 110
upset 64
utter 29
utterly 35, 75

V

vacantly 1, 97, 100, 105
vague 95, 105
vast 74, 95, 101
veering 27
verdant 1
very 67
vexed 22, 102
vibration 48
viscous 67, 71
vivid 78
vividly 2, 5, 101

W

waaa 6
waah 110
waddling 108
wailing 1, 6, 79
warm 96, 101
warmly 98
warping 87
wavering 90
weakly 68, 94
wearily 30
weeping 104
well-done 36
welling 40
wet 42, 70
whack 73-74, 77
wham 11, 73
whiff 88

whining 10, 19, 28, 32, 40
whirling 28, 84
whishing 83
whispering 38, 81
whistle 83
whistling 45, 83
white 8
whoa 63
wholly 25, 49, 50, 66
whonk 14
whoosh 95
whump 63
wide 8, 28, 47, 107
wide open 77
wide-open 97
winding 5, 26
withered 24
wobbly 8, 27
wordy 24
worried 107
worrying 27
wrestle 41
wriggle 3, 41
wriggling 69, 106
writhe 3

Y

yapping 19
yelling 19
yelping 19, 36

Z

zig-zag 40
zing 20
zinging 17
zong 30
zunk 30

TOYO PRess: Explore Dream Discover

Editorial supervision: Dominique Giovannangeli. Book and cover design: Chōkei Studios. Printing and binding: IngramSpark. The typefaces used are Osaka and Trebuchet MS.

www.ingramcontent.com/pod-product-compliance
Lightning Source LLC
Chambersburg PA
CBHW050241010526
44107CB00040B/1474/J